HISTORY OF CANAL IRRIGATION IN COASTAL ORISSA: 1866-1947

ABOUT THE AUTHOR

Baira Ganjan Dash teaches history at Dhamnagar College (Bhadrak), Fakir Mohan University. He is an emerging historian.

HISTORY OF CANAL IRRIGATION IN COASTAL ORISSA: 1866-1947

Baira Ganjan Dash

CONCEPT PUBLISHING COMPANY PVT. LTD.
NEW DELHI-110059

ISBN-13: 978-93-88937-44-3

First Published 2020

Published and Printed by

Concept Since 1974

Concept Publishing Company Pvt. Ltd.
A/15-16, Commercial Block, Mohan Garden,
New Delhi-110059 (INDIA)
T: 91 11 25351460, 91 11 25351794
E: publishing@conceptpub.com; *W*: www.conceptpub.com

Cataloging in Publication Data--Courtesy: D.K. Agencies (P) Ltd. <docinfo@dkagencies.com>

Dash, Baira Ganjan, author
History of canal irrigation in coastal Orissa: 1866-1947 / Baira Ganjan Dash.
pages cm

"...originally written as part of his M.Phil degree dissertation at the Department of History, Sikkim University, Gangtok in 2017"—Foreword.
Includes bibliographical references and index.
ISBN 9789388937443

1. Irrigation—India—Odisha—History. 2. Irrigation canals and flumes—India—Odisha—History. 3. Peasants—India—Odisha—History. 4. Agriculture—Economic aspects—India—Odisha—History. I. Title.

LCC TC903.D37 2019 | DDC 627.520954133 23

Dedicated
To

Mother – Chanchala Dash
&
Father Late Jagabandhu Das
and
Dr. T. Vijay kumar
Dr. V. Krishna Ananth

With respect

Foreword

History of Canal Irrigation in Castal Orissa: 1866-1947 by Baira Ganjan Dash, was originally written as part of his M.Phil degree dissertation at the Department of History, Sikkim University, Gangtok, in 2017. I must commend Baira for having chosen to work on a dissertation on such a topic in times when research in our universities are drifting towards aspects of cultural theory. Economic history, one of the key areas of the discipline, demanding rigours of a high order is rarely a subject matter of research in our times. Baira decided to go against the fashion and I am happy to introduce this publication for this and a variety of reasons.

This book, which is a far more improved version of his dissertation will serve its purpose as a highly accessible illustration of Marxist historical method on the colonial irrigation system of coastal Orissa in the colonial period. The importance of the book lies in the fact that it could serve as the basis to further studies of this kind on the colonial irrigation system.

The book will also serve as an important model with immense value to anyone seeking to engage in research of the kind that we now address in the academia as area studies. Baira's access and selection of sources, primary for most parts, is indeed what makes this relevant. The most striking feature of this book, in my view, is the interconnection he makes between the enlargement/expansion of the various canals and its impact on the agrarian economy and agrarian market, all of these in the colonial context.

The extensive use of primary sources, culled from the Odisha State Archives with meticulous care and effort, has helped in constructing a very good picture of all changes brought about by the canal irrigation constructed by the colonial administration. It is simply written and therefore will be accessible to those seeking to study and make sense of the colonial project in the making of the irrigation system in coastal Orissa.

Dr. V. Krishna Ananth,
Associate Professor, Department of History,
Sikkim University, Gangtok

February 18, 2019

Acknowledgements

In the two years over which this book gestated, developed, and culminated, I have received support and solidarity from many, many people. It is impossible to thank them individually. My apologies, but I presume they know who they are.

At the same time, I would like to begin by thanking Dr. T. Vijay Kumar, Associate Professor and Head, Department of History, Sikkim University whose expertise and interest in agrarian history has contributed enormously to the present work without which the work would not have been completed. I express my deepest gratitude to Dr. V. Krishna Ananth, Associate Professor, Department of History, Sikkim University and E.K. Santha, Research Scholar, Department of History, Sikkim University for their suggestions in improving the work and also for their moral support.

Nothing will suffice to express my indebtedness to my family members (Father—Late Mr. Jagabandhu Dash and Mother Smt. Chanchala Dash, my Brother Sri Rudra Narayan Dash and sister Rajalaxmi Dash) for their continuous insistence that I should go for higher studies despite all the difficulties they had to face in the process. They always encouraged my studies without letting me to know about their sufferings. I am also indebted to parent like figure Nayana Mallick, former Head, Department of History, Bhadrak Autonomous College, Bhadrak and Dr. Khirod Ch. Mallick, English Reader, Bhadrak Autonomous College for their kind cooperation.

I am thankful to Sankar Narayan Bagh, Assistant Professor,

Department of Sociology, Sikkim University for his invaluable cooperation. I acknowledge the help rendered by Dr. Rasmi Satpathy, librarian of Orissa State Archives in accessing primary materials from the archives for the present work.

Finally, my thanks are due to Sri Tamila Paraseth, Lecturer in Political Science, Gunupur College, Rayagada, Orissa, Sri Tikelal Mehar, Lecturer in Economics, G.P.R. College, Kuntara, Sambalpur, Orissa, Sheikh Ansar Ali, Biplove Kumar, Deepmoni Gogoi, Ugen Bhutia, Research Scholars in the Department of History, Sikkim University and Abdulla Khandakar, Research Scholar, Department of Sociology, Sikkim University for their academic assistance.

Baira Ganjan Dash

Contents

List of Figures and Tables

LIST OF FIGURES

LIST OF TABLES

Abbreviations

AGAROD	:	Annual General Administration Report of the Orissa Division
AGROD	:	Annual General Report of Orissa Divi sion
BODG	:	Bihar and Orissa District Gazetteers
EIICC	:	East India Irrigation and Canal Company
GAROD	:	General Administration Report on Orissa Division
RABO	:	Report on the Administration of Bihar and Orissa
SCRO	:	Season and Crop Report of Orissa

Introduction

During the colonial period, Coastal Colonial Orissa mainly comprised of three districts, i.e. Cuttack, Puri and Balasore districts. They were situated on the east coast of India along the Bay of Bengal. The coastal Orissa was highly fertile in nature and plain. Its relation with Bengal was much closer than any other areas of colonial India. In 1803, Orissa passed from the hands of the Marathas to the British hands. Till 1905, Northern Orissa comprised of the above mentioned districts. In 1936, based on the language, Orissa was formed with six districts namely; three Coastal districts of Cuttack, Puri and Balasore, two southern districts Ganjam and Koraput and western district of Sambalpur.

The havoc played by the flood in 1855 attracted the attention of the British to this region and they began to gather expert opinions in order to mitigate the intermittent floods that affected Orissa severely. Capt. Harris was the one who proposed to construct channels to drain the surplus water that was emerged during the flood time. In addition to this, Arthur Cotton, an Engineer from Madras Presidency further proposed to construct canals for twin purposes: to irrigate the land and also for navigational purpose.[1] However, the immediate provocation was the great famine that hit Orissa in 1866. It played havoc on the human and other resources in the region. It was the same year that the British decided to invest on the canal system in Orissa. Hence, 1866 was a significant year in the history of Orissa. It changed the political economy of Orissa extensively.

Subsequently, Orissa had witnessed the construction of some major canals like, the Orissa Coast Canal, the Taladanda Canal, the Kendrapada Canal, the Pattamundai Canal and others. However; the process of the expansion of canal irrigation was very slow. Firstly, the people were reluctant with the new concept and also were apprehensive about the idea of water tax. Secondly, the annual rainfall in Orissa was adequate in most of the times.[2] They had to depend on the canal for irrigation only when the monsoon failed. For these reasons, the process of canal expansion took a longer period of time. Once it was completed, the canals became yet another source of income to the British. Over a period, they collected a huge sum by canal as the water tax and navigational charges.

The policies of the British, beginning from the land tenure system to tax pattern, were not favourable for the peasants. One of the direct impact of the canal irrigation system was that with the extension of canal irrigation people belonged to the Coastal Orissa lost their which lead to the loss of self-dependency. For instance, Sohini Sengupta pointed out that with the loss of traditional water sources in western Orissa, people of that region had felt the loss of self-independency, which was due to the eradication of some old inherited provisions, such as the abolition of landlordship and free labour system.[3] It was the sole assumption of the colonialists that canal irrigation was the only cause for the expansion of agriculture, but it has been proved that the canal irrigation accompanied by population increase and their demand for more production brought little changes in the agriculture sector. But in real sense there was no expansion of agriculture as the common peasant was made to believe; but the peasants suffered in many ways. A time, the water tax was unaffordable to the farmers and the good rainfalls were the only saving grace. Some of the policies of the British were responsible for the destruction of Coastal Orissa's agricultural sector to a large extent. And still those adverse effects were apparent in the region.

With the entry of the British into Orissa in 1803, the policy of political aggrandisement started. They began to interfere in every matter; agriculture was not an exception. By their intervention, it went under a new phase of colonization which could be called in other words as colonisation of agriculture. In other words, through the measures such as new land revenue system, new landownership law, commercial crops, canal irrigation system, and water tax and so on, the British colonised Orissa's agriculture. And this process of colonization accentuated with the construction of canals. The Oriya peasants succumbed to the pressure that was exerted by British. Probably canal was the last aspect that threw the Oriya peasants into a market economy.

There were historians belonged to the Imperialistic School such as Morris D. Morris and W.H. Moreland, who argued that the British intervention improved the agriculture sector considerably.[4] In their study they maintained that per capita agricultural production increased. Perceived from the international market price for agricultural produce, they asserted that Indian peasants now got chance to maximize their income. But the peasants never enjoyed that profit for the simple reason that it did not reach them. On the contrary, the heavy tax burden and the compulsory cultivation of commercial crops brought sufferings to the peasants.[5] The cultivation of commercial crops was thrust up on the peasants as it provided raw materials for the British. Yet, another lacuna of their study was that they did not calculate that rise of population was one of the pushing factors for the rise of agriculture. Back to the construction of canals, this was one of ways to maximise their profit. But it was projected as Good Samaritan activity by the British; mitigate the floods and provide irrigation facilities to the farmers in the region.

Profit was always the disguised intention of the colonialists. Wherever the British did not get much profit they did not concentrate too much and left that aspect.[6] The British introduced canal irrigation in Orissa on the pretext to protect agriculture from flood and famines. In this disguise, they constructed the canal system. But collected huge revenue out of it through water tax and navigation charges. When they increased the water tax; the peasants in Orissa suffered unjustifiably. Because of the high taxation system there was nothing left with the peasants. It is evident from the fact that till independence the economic condition of the Orissa peasants remained the same or worse than before. Both the landlords and the British officers exacted from the common peasants through a number of ways that led to untold miseries to the Orissa peasants.

In course of time, the indifference of the British towards the maintenance of existing traditional water sources grew as these did not bring any gain to them, led to the decline of the traditional water sources in Orissa. Taking side with the locallords, the British also contributed to the substantial decrease in the number of traditional water sources. And the extension of canals made the process of decline of those sources very fast. Once the peasants were assessed for water tax, they were compelled to pay tax; whether or not they availed canal facility or not. The British also did not bother, whether canal water reached to the peasant's farmland or not.

Yet another development was that, with the construction of canals, the commercialisation of agriculture also made an entry to Orissa. It is true that there were references of the cultivation of commercial crops in the nineteenth century documents, it was not in large scale cultivation, or it was not intended to satisfy the need of the market but to cater the local needs. The cultivation of jute and sugarcane for local need are good examples. The process of commercialisation of agriculture began with the demand of land revenue in cash.[7] This was once again backed by the high amount of additional water tax. Now, the Orissa peasants produced not for themselves but for markets. The subsistence nature of agriculture turned into commercial agriculture. It was always claimed that it was the need of the people to maximise their income behind the commercial crops cultivation. But not for the profit which was promised by the cash crops but to meet the heavy demand of taxes (both land tax and water tax), the peasants began to cultivate commercial crops in large scale. It is also true the British adopted a tactics initially to attract the peasants to the commercial crops; they cut the water rate. This was also done with the intension of popularising canal irrigation system among the peasants.

The more the peasants used of the canal water, the more it brought revenue to the British. And this was one among many other causes for the underdevelopment of Orissa's agriculture. Sometimes, the canal irrigation system displeased the intermediaries also, because they used to get scared of the high demand of revenue imposed by the British to be exacted from the peasants. The heavy amount of tax burden along with several other agricultural policies displeased the peasants so much so that peasants even went against the British, which resulted in popular peasant risings. The dissatisfaction of the peasants and the related uprisings can be seen in the contemporary literatures.

According to the British, water tax was very low; still the peasants were hesitant to draw water from the canals. The British accused the Orissa peasants being ignorant, conservative and were not ready to accept any kind of development in the field of agriculture. The British, however, admitted the fact that, the water rates, most of the times, were unaffordable to the farmers; there were mismanagement inside the massive canal administrative system. They also neglected that fact that the peasants were not happy with the arrangements and for them the canal irrigation was just a fall-back during a drought due to low rainfall. On the trade and commerce front, a new chapter began with the opening of canal system. Now, communication improved a step forward from bullock cart to canal as was the rightly pointed by the colonialists. In this aspect they should be thanked. Transferring of goods became much easier than before. This increased export of agricultural products of Orissa to other provinces or states within the British India. Ultimately, Orissa market system was colonised and brought under the direct supervision of the colonialists; this needless to say that, ousted the existing indigenous market system such as *hats*. Simultaneously, canal waterways ensured an additional income to the British namely the navigational income. This further accentuated the urbanization process with this emerged new towns and cities with new features of market.

No serious attempt has been made so far to study background for the introduction of canal irrigation and the British canals impact on coastal districts of colonial Orissa. This humble effort is a step in opening the hidden impacts of British canal irrigation method.

Much before the existing historiography of Orissa Canal system, the colonial historiography of canal system claimed that canal irrigation had brought all positive result for colonial India. For example, Bernard Darley, a knighthood awardee and from 1919 until 1931 he was Chief Engineer to the Sarda Canal irrigation project, posed a statement that represented one of the early colonial centric stands. In his argument, he argued that by introducing canal project, the British was able to reclaim vast stretched waste land which was an admirable work for the peasants of India. Along with that he also argued that canal irrigation system brought all kinds of modernization in the field of agriculture in general and irrigation in particular. This notion of statement he prepared in his work, *The Development of Irrigation in India.*[8] Like colonial historiography, the Cambridge historiography of canal irrigation also supported the colonial claim of improvement of agriculture. The best example of the Cambridge school of historiography was Ian Stone's work on canal irrigation. Ian Stone argued that because of canal system modernization came in the agrarian sector of India. Peasants got chance of agricultural protection from scanty rainfall and heavy floods. Production increased some extent. New lands were brought under the cultivation for the first time by the canal irrigation. Peasants were happy under the modern canal system.[9]

Like colonial or Cambridge historiography, the existing historiography of Orissa Canal system of Orissa stands on the same idea of improvement of agriculture because of canal irrigation. Most of the historians of Orissa have admired the introduction of canal irrigation in Colonial Orissa. The main causes for their admiration were that the development of agriculture and navigation to which they attributed to the British canal system.

Specifically speaking, Jaya Krushna Samal, an eminent scholar in the field of economic history who first looked at the agrarian prospect in a clear-cut manner in his works such as, *Economy of Colonial Orissa, 1866-1947, Economic History of Orissa, 1866-1912,* and *Agrarian History of Orissa under the British Rule.*[10] In his opinion he boldly maintained his argument that canal irrigation changed the face of agriculture of Colonial Coastal Orissa by bringing modernization in agriculture. His reason of admiration to the canal system was, the improvement of navigational aspect and some extent, it saved crop. But he remained silent on the issue of canal's real impacts on the Coastal Colonial Orissa. In the same way like Jay Krushna Samal, Purna Chandra Das in his work, *The Economic History of Orissa in the 19th Century* maintained his position by raising the opinion that with the introduction of the British canal system agriculture developed.[11] Similar kind of stand was taken by Gorachand Pattnaik in his work, *The Famine and Some Aspects of the British Economic Policy in Orissa, 1866-1905*[12], in this matter of admiration without much looking to canal's role in bringing negative impacts on coastal Orissa. Subash Chandra Bhola in his work, *British Economic Policy in Orissa, 1905-1947,* went a step ahead in his argument. He argued that the newly devised canal system had all kinds of benefits along with protection from floods and famines. Or indirectly it could be said that he attributed protective nature to the British canals. For him also the canal irrigation served as a medium for the improvement of agriculture and communication by the way of navigation.[13] Once again by arguing so, Bhola made the earlier argument very strong. But Ratna Sahoo's argument was slightly different from what earlier was proposed in relation to the canal irrigation. While all perceived that it was the canal irrigation played a major role behind the development of agriculture, but Ratna Sahoo in addition to the older propositions argued that along with the canal irrigation, increased population and other government initiatives were responsible. Overall her argument was that canal irrigation was one of the positive attempt of the British which she maintained in her work, *Agricultural Development in British Orissa.*[14] Avaya Kumar

Behera's article, *Irrigation in British Orissa* argued that though with the canal irrigation agriculture developed but due to the rise of the cost of living there was nothing much left with the peasants as profit.[15] So, overall speaking all the historians have supported the canal irrigation.

But, on the contrary to the Cambridge and colonial historiography, Elizabeth Withcombe, for the first time in her article on "Irrigation" brought a new insight of dissatisfaction of the peasants due to the canal irrigation. Elizabeth argued that because of canal irrigation the problem of salinity came, health problem aroused along with fertility loss of agricultural lands. In addition to this, Elizabeth also argued the canal system was responsible for the decline of traditional water sources in India.[16] This argument was later on proved to be very true in the context of Andhra region in general and Krishna district in particular by G.N. Rao. In his article "*Transition from subsistence to commercial agriculture: A study of Krishna district of Andhra, 1850-1900*",[17] he also argued because of modern method of irrigation system the nature of subsistence of production had been turned into commercial production. Along with that he also argued the commercial crops cultivation increased to large extent with the entry of the modern form of irrigational system. There was water management problem along with the problem of water distribution in the modern method of irrigation to which, he vehemently opposed. In this context, the argument of Nirmal Sengupta in his article *Irrigation: Traditional vs. modern*"[18] has much value. In his write-up he argued traditional irrigational systems were simpler in management, environmental friendly and less wastage of agricultural lands.

Interestingly, the Imperialist notion of modernization was fired back by David Gilmartin, in his work *Scientific Empire and Imperial Science: Colonialism and Irrigation Technology in the Indus Basin.*[19] As per his argument by the application of science, the British wanted to justify their rule over colony. Canal irrigation gave them the power of dictation over irrigation and agriculture too. He also admitted the appearance of environmental problems because of the arrival of canal irrigation.

Ganeswar Nayak in his work *The Coast Canal in Orissa during the colonial era*[20] discussed its construction and extension. His write up does bear any stand. Sohini Sengupta's work *Political Economy of Irrigation, Tanks in Orissa, 1850-1996*[21], was on the western Orissa particularly. In her work she argued with the abolition of lordship system (*Gountia,* village head) the number of wells declined rapidly as they were the ones who used to contribute finance for the traditional water source's management. And also they were the ones who used to lead the peasants for traditional water sources management. Hence her work contributes the fact that the local lords were the preservers of traditional water sources.

But the real situation because of the canal irrigation in Coastal Orissa was something other, as same as Elizabeth Withcombe's and G.N. Rao's argument partially which were not explored out by the historians of Orissa. Peasants' dissatisfaction was there too much in the colonial Coastal Orissa. The system brought so many changes in the agrarian trade and agrarian market. But, the above book reviews in relation to the canal irrigation system of colonial Coastal Orissa clearly shows that there is a gap in the discussion on the impact of canal system in coastal Orissa. In order to understand this historical process, it is essential as well as it is justified here to have an introspective study in this matter.

In this study an attempt has been made to bring a full-fledged understanding on how traditional water sources were ruined with the opening of canal irrigation and also other long term consequences of the canal irrigation. The present work aims at presenting for the first time a detailed, dispassionate, and analytical study of some very important questions like how Orissa peasants were dissatisfied with the British canal system and why Orissa became an agrarian colony for the colonialists in the course of time.

The present study aims at looking for the study of different types of traditional water sources in coastal Orissa for the period 1866-1947, to reconstruct the whole course of the extension of canal irrigation in coastal Orissa during colonial period, to analyse its impact on agrarian economy and agrarian market.

The study has been carried out with the help of primary sources and secondary sources collected from various archives and libraries. And the study was conducted from the point of view of the peasant and priority has been given to project their voice in order to understand the real situation against the claims of the colonial historians, which was totally ignored from their opinion. Oriya literature sources were to highlight the discontent of the poor peasants of those times. The yearly statistical data has been used extensively for the analysis. The time series data analysis was made to understand the extension of canal irrigation, extension of cultivation, irrigational revenue, and navigational income and so on. For easy understanding of the historical progress of irrigation and canal extension, graphic presentation and data tables are given.

Notes

1. *Report of the Irrigation Rates Revision Committee*, Government of Orissa, 1967, pp. 6-7.
2. Hunter, W. (1872). *Orissa* (Vol. II), London: Smith, Elder & Co., p. 175.
3. Sengupta, S. (2000). "Political Economy of Irrigation: Tanks in Orissa, 1850-1996", *Economic and Political Weekly*, 2000, December 30, pp. 4695-4700.
4. Chandra, B. (1999). *Essays on Colonialism,* New Delhi: Orient Blackswan Private Limited, pp. 127-128.
5. Mukherjee, Mridula (2005). *Colonizing Agriculture: The Myth of Punjab Exceptionalism,* New Delhi: Sage Publication India Private Limited.
6. Reddy, M.A. (1990). "Travails of an Irrigation Company in South India", *Economic and Political Weekly, Vol. 25* (no. 12), 619-621+623-628, March.
7. Das, B.S. (1976). "Orissa's Economy in the Nineteenth Century", *Social Scientist,* Vol. 4 (No. 11), June, pp. 40-42.

8. Darley, Bernard (1941). "The Development of Irrigation in India", *Journal of the Royal Society of Arts,* 90 (4602): 39-56, December 12.
9. Stone, Ian (1984). *Canal Irrigation in British India: Perspectives on Technological Change in a Peasant Economy*. London: Cambridge University Press.
10. Samal, J.K. (2000). *Economic History of Colonial Orissa, 1866-1947,* New Delhi: Munshiram Manohar Publishers Pvt. Ltd.; *Economic History of Orissa (1866-1912),* New Delhi: Mittal Publications, 1990; *Agrarian History of Orissa Under the British Rule,* Delhi: Kanishka Publishers Distributers, 1993.
11. Das, P.C. (1989). *The Economic History of Orissa in the 19th Century,* New Delhi: Commonwealth Publisher.
12. Patnaik, G. (1980). *The Famine and Some Aspects of the British Economic Policy in Orissa (1866-1905),* Vidyapuri, Cuttack.
13. Bhola, S.C. (1990). *British Economic Policy in Orissa (1905-1947),* New Delhi: Discovery Publishing House.
14. Sahoo, R. (1997). "Agricultural Development in British Orissa", (Ed.), N.R. Patnaik, *Economic History of Orissa,* New Delhi: Indus Publishing House.
15. Behera, A.K. (1997). "Irrigation in British Orissa", (Ed.), N.R. Patnaik, *Economic History of Orissa,* New Delhi: Indus Publishing Company.
16. Whitcombe, Elizabeth, (1984). "Irrigation", In: D. Kumar, M. Desai, and S. Bhattacharya *The Cambridge Economic History of India* (Vol. II, pp. 677-737), New Delhi: Orient Longman Private Limited.
17. Rao, G.N. "Transition from Subsistence to Commercialised Agriculture: A Study of Krishna District of Andhra", *Economic and Political Weekly,* Vol. 20 (No. 25/26), A60-A69, 1985, June 22-29.
18. Sengupta, N. "Irrigation: Traditional *vs* Modern", *Economic and Political Weekly,* Vol. 20 (No. 45/47), 1919-1921+1923-1925+1927+1929-1931+1933+1935+1937-1938, 1985, November.
19. Gilmartin, D. (1994). "Scientific Empire and Imperial Science: Colonialism and Irrigation Technology in the Indus Basin", *The Journal of Asian Studies,* Vol. 53 (No. 4), November.
20. Nayak, G. (2010). "The Coast Canal in Orissa during the Colonial Era", *Orissa Review,* May-June, *Orissa Review,* May-June.
21. Sengupta, S. (2000). "Political Economy of Irrigation: Tanks in Orissa, 1850-1996", *Economic and Political Weekly,* December 30.

1
Changes in the Traditional Irrigation System and its Impact on Peasantry

> If a person stops to irrigate land from a conventional water source or prepares a new water source instead of using the running old one, which cannot be used to carry out conventional works, then the person would be punished severely.
> *Arthashastra*[1]

> The Oriya is a very conservative cultivator and has an apathetic indifference to agricultural improvements.
> *L.S.S. O'Malley*[2]

The economy of Orissa was built around agriculture. Agriculture was and still it is the mainstay of Orissa economy. In Orissa over 90 per cent of the population was dependant on agriculture directly and indirectly, as it was its main means of livelihood.[3] Agriculture took care of almost all the basic needs of the Orissa people. It also helped to sustain non-agricultural activities of economy like, manufacture sector, trade and commerce and transport. In the past, availability of water was one of the most important components for carrying out agriculture activities. It is the same even today. However, at present only 28.90 per cent of the land in Orissa covers with irrigational facilities where around 60 per cent of people are still involved.[4] Lack of sufficient water sources to irrigate Orissa's agricultural land has deep impact on the Orissa's economy. However, this problem is not a newly emerged one but it was there since the British age itself. In other words, the British were responsible for this crisis, as they did not pay their attention to preserve and improve the existing traditional water sources. On the contrary, they mainly paid their attention on canal irrigation which in a way caused the loss of these traditional sources.

Since the ancient time, Orissa had developed its own system of irrigation feeling its imperativeness as the region depended on monsoon rains and was exposed to the risk of famines and droughts. It is noteworthy that these traditional irrigation systems, that were created to irrigate the agricultural land, were geographically suitable and environmentally viable. The traditional irrigation systems were very good in terms of simpler management (community), less wastage of cultivable land and also for environmental reasons.[5] The introduction of new method of irrigation system by the British destroyed the traditional system irrevocably and the community management, which was an important element of the traditional system replaced by officialdom. Earlier the farmers were independent, in the sense, they irrigated their land according to their will and need. Planning of traditional water sources, construction, management, and water distribution was in the hands of peasants as a whole.[6] Whatever may be traditional irrigation pattern, it had its own uniqueness in the agrarian history.

DIFFERENT KINDS OF TRADITIONAL IRRIGATIONAL SOURCES

Before going into the changes that took place in the traditional irrigation systems, it is pertinent to have a look at the different kinds of traditional irrigational sources that were existed throughout colonial Coastal Orissa.

First and foremost, Oriya peasants depended more on rains for the cultivation of their land. Around 70 per cent of the land was cultivated through this natural source. Remaining 30 per cent was cultivated through irrigation using traditional kind of irrigation system. Only in the exceptional years peasants used to go for artificial irrigation methods. Coming to traditional artificial irrigation, specifically, various forms of sources were used in this regard. Such were (a) from rivers by means of water lifts; (b) by damming up natural streams; (c) from tanks (*garhias*); (d) from natural springs; and (e) from wells.[7]

In Puri district, very big tanks were dug up for irrigation purpose. During rainy season, those big tanks were filled with water, as every tank used to absorb all the drained water of that area. In addition to this, streams were also made use to irrigate the agricultural land in Puri district in general and Khorda region of Puri district in particular.[8] Side by side irrigation used to take place in this Khorda region both from natural rainfall and perennial springs. However, even these sources were insufficient to irrigate the whole region and hence, the peasants of that region used to depend on the tanks and the water of streams and numerous *nullahs* (small water channels).[9] Some tanks were natural origin; many others were dug by the local peasants. In the plain areas of the district rivers formed the main sources of irrigation for the agricultural lands. Small drains were constructed to reach the river water to the agricultural lands.[10]

Similarly in the Cuttack district river irrigation system was the pivotal irrigation method. Among the rivers the Mahanadi, Kathajodi, and Brahmani were the main water sources.[11] Different water lifting methods were used to lift the water of those rivers to the agricultural land.[12] And side by side tanks were also used as another irrigational source.[13] Wells, and streams were the other chief source of irrigation.[14]

Balasore district was not at all exception to this. There was not much need of the digging of tanks because of sufficient rainfall.[15] Still wells and tanks were used as water sources.

It was very common practice among the Orissa peasants to dig small tanks near to a cluster of their agricultural lands. Whenever its water was desired, particularly at the time of scanty rainfall they used to draw water from it according to their need.[16] Interestingly, digging such tanks or creating a water resource was considered as a sacred work by the Orissa peasants, particularly by all sections of tribal, as it combined some sort of humanity. Orissa peasants were supposedly, expert in the art of the digging tanks. Their expertise was well-known so as they were invited frequently by far area people to do so.[17]

As far as stream irrigation was concerned, small check dams were generally built across natural streams, in order to raise water level to a little higher level. The raised water either flow directly from the river to the agricultural land or it was brought through the small artificial channels, locally called as *pahanis* (very small water channels) created by the peasants.[18] In most parts of Orissa, irrigation from streams was mainly required for paddy in the month of October and November.[19] Its water was mainly used in the fields of sugarcane, tobacco, cotton, and paddy during the colonial period.[20]

Coming to tanks, tanks were generally of two kinds. Some could be described as ordinary and others were special, according to its quality. The ordinary ones were dug not so big and deep and were occasionally fed by natural springs. Special ones were constructed of the embankments across sloping land. Those embankments never allowed the above land to be intercepted. Sometimes by the use of labour force, the tanks were made deeper than the normal with intention to enhance the capacity to retain more water. Sometimes, these kinds of tanks were also fed by natural springs.[21] When the modern form of canal irrigation was introduced, the tank water was used for paddy land irrigation, in the month of October and November.[22] However, during the British period its water was mainly used for the cultivation of sugarcane, tobacco, cotton, and paddy.[23] But its role in the matter of irrigation was very significant.

Wells were yet another most important water source, as far as the private irrigation works were concerned.[24] Wells were mostly used in the fields of garden crops and betel plantations.[25] It was also used for sugarcane and potatoes cultivation along with paddy fields during the colonial period.[26] Citing the importance of the wells in the context of agriculture in Orissa, the Famine Commission of 1945 viewed: "Wells are a most important source of irrigation and if the area under irrigation is to expand to the fullest extent, a large increase in the numbers of private wells is imperative."[27]

Besides, all the above water sources there were also private canals during the colonial period. Those canals were considered as private because those were constructed by medieval rulers of Orissa. Private canals continued its existence till even 1947, which has been proved from different season and crop reports.

To some extent irrigation was also carried on by means of water lifts. For example *dalua*, hot weather crops and some sugarcane cultivation. In order to raise the water level from a lower level to higher level special contrivances were used. Those special devises were called as *tenda*, *sena* and *janta* were specially designed or invented to draw water from lower lands.[28]

Tenda is consisted of two upright posts with a cross bar, which used to serve as a fulcrum on which a bamboo pole works; the latter was weighted at one end by a stone or mass of mud, and at the other a thin bamboo was fastened, with an earthen pot or bucket attached. Whenever water was required the cultivator used to pull down the bamboo pole till the bucket was immersed. As soon as the task was over, the weight attached to the lever raised the bucket of itself, and the water was then emptied into a pipe, which was generally the hollowed trunk of a palm tree, and was directed into the fields, through narrow channels. Whenever, the field was considerable higher than the water, a platform was built on four stout bamboos on which a man stands to work the lever.[29]

Sena was a yet another device which was used to raise water a few feet. It was a sort of basket made of split bamboo, which was used by two men. Holding the ropes attached to either side, they used to swing it backward, and used to bring it down very sharply into the water carried forward motion of the swing through, until the basket got full of water, was raised to the level of the water channel, when the contents were poured out.[30]

The third contrivance for lifting water to a short distance was *janta*. It was made of a single piece of wood about ten feet long.[31] Sometimes, it was only six feet long.[32] It was hollowed out and shaped like one-half of a canoe. The broad open end generally used to be placed on the head of a water channel. This pointed closed end used to be put into the water, and when this was raised, the water poured naturally into the water channel. This kind of job was generally done by one man. This device had limited capacity.[33]

Besides above methods, the peasantry of the region also used earthen pots in lifting the water from one place to other. It was locally known as *mathia*. This was a strenuous and time taking process considering the fact that the Orissa peasants used to carry it to a considerable distance. Mainly it was done in the case of valuable crops.[34]

It was unfortunate that there were no records available on the number of tanks, wells and other traditional sources that existed in the pre-independent period. However, the limited available sources pertaining to this area will be analysed. During the agricultural year 1939-40, in Cuttack district only, 32,038 acres of land was irrigated by tanks whereas from wells 395 acres of land was irrigated. And from other sources it was 20,573 acres excluding government canal sources. In the same year, the total land under private canals was 16,630 acres.[35] It was around 24.91 per cent of the total irrigated land. In 1941-42, 40,000 acres of land was irrigated from tanks. From wells it was 700 acres, whereas from other sources it was 30,000 acres. However, around 20,000 acres of land was under the private canals.[36] It could be observed from the statistics that the well irrigation was almost doubled from 395 acres in 1939-40 to 700 acres in 1941-42 period; other sources also marked a considerable increase. There is a marginal increase in tank irrigation too. The total share of the traditional irrigation was 29.94 per cent of the total irrigated land. But in 1943-44 in the same district from tanks, around 34,600 acres of land was irrigated. Wells once again commanded over 700 acres. Private canals commanded over 18,400 acres of land. From other sources excluding canal irrigated lands, 28,800 acres of land was irrigated.[37] This was less than the period 1941-42. Its share out of the total irrigated land was 26 per cent. In 1944-45 periods, tanks stood out at the forefront of major traditional irrigational sources. It commanded over 36,800 acres of land. Next to it, the wells also irrigated around 1,300 acres of land. By means of other traditional sources, 34,700 acres of agricultural land was irrigated. Comparing to previous year, in this year private canals commanded over 19,300 acres of land, which was slight rise.[38] Now, by that year traditional sources contribution to the total irrigated land was 27.94 per cent. But by 1945-46 its share rose to 30.30 per cent. It was so because, the total acres of the irrigated land increased from the tanks and reached to 40,840 acres. Similarly, the number of acres of land irrigated through well irrigation also increased to 2,700 acres and from other traditional sources 36,700 acres of land was irrigated. And 18,700 acres of land was under the private canal irrigation.[39] (*see* Table 1.1)

The available statistics for the Balasore district goes like this. In 1939-40, the total land irrigated by tanks was 1,300 acres. From other sources excluding government canal system was 1,500 acres. Private canal system commanded 980 acres of land.[40] Its share to the total irrigated land of Balasore was 11.49 per cent. During 1941-42, tanks and wells together irrigated land was 2,000 acres, whereas from other sources excluding government canals it was 400 acres. Around 930 acres of land was under the command of private canal system.[41] Now, the share of traditional irrigation to total irrigated land dropped to 11.28 per cent. The same amount of land was irrigated during 1943-44[42], but the share was again reduced to 11.13 per cent. For the year 1944-45, tanks and wells together irrigated over 2,132 acres of land. The other sources irrigated over 468 acres of land, whereas private canals commanded over 930 acres of agricultural land.[43] In that particular year, the share of traditional irrigation rose to 11.72 per cent. During 1945-46, around 1,108 acres of land was irrigated by tank system and from wells it was 1,250 acres of land. By private canals only 930 acres of land was irrigated. From other sources only

Table 1.1: The Extent of Cultivation under various traditional Irrigational system from 1939-40 to 1945-46 (*in acres*)

Year	Cuttack				Balasore				Puri			
	Tanks	Wells	Other Irrigational sources	Private canals	Tanks	Wells	Other Irrigational sources	Private canals	Tanks	Wells	Other Irrigational sources	Private canals
1939-40	32,038	395	20,573	16,630	1,300	—	1,500	980	51,600	2,500	1,47,250	15,000
1941-42	40,000	700	30,000	20,000	2,000	—	400	930	51,600	2,500	1,47,250	15,000
1943-44	34,600	700	28,800	18,400	2,000	—	400	930	51,600	2,500	1,47,595	15,000
1944-45	36,800	1,300	34,700	19,300	2,132	—	468	930	51,660	2,500	1,47,967	15,000
1945-46	40,840	2,700	36,700	18,730	1,108	1,250	562	930	51,660	2,500	1,48,178	5,000

Source: Season and Crop Reports of Orissa for the Years 1939-40 to 1945-46.

562 acres of land was irrigated in that particular year.[44] There was increase from the previous period. Now, the total share of the traditional irrigation rose up to 12.65 per cent.

Like the other districts discussed above, in Puri district also available statistics is far and few. During the period 1939-40, the total area irrigated by tank system was 51,600 acres. The wells irrigated 2,500 acres of land and Private canals irrigated around 1,500 acres of land. Other sources excluding canal system commanded over 1,47,250 acres of land.[45] Comparing to other districts in Puri district had highest share in this regard. Particularly in 1939-40, its total contribution to total irrigated land was 100 per cent. In the agricultural year of 1941-42, the same amount of land was irrigated from the same each irrigational sources.[46] Hence, the total share was the same as of 1939-40. But in 1943-44, its share raised some extent because of the little rise of irrigated land to 1,47,595 acres by other sources excluding government canals way.[47] Otherwise other sources like tanks and wells irrigated over the same amount of land as was in the preceding years. In that particular year, the share of traditional irrigation was 100 per cent. Followed by in 1944-45, the tank irrigation covered an addition of 60 more acres of land. Now the amount touched to 51,660 acres of land. Along with that the private canals share was 1,500 acres of land. Similarly in the section of other sources excluding canal system, little rise was seen and the total irrigated land was 1,47,967 acres.[48] Hence, the total share was the same as the previous years, 100 per cent. Followed by in 1945-1946, there was only change in the section of other source which showed little decline in the irrigation sector. The amount of irrigated land was 1,48,178 acres. Along with that private canals share was 5,000 acres of land.[49] However, in that year the total contribution of traditional water sources to the total irrigated land was 95.39 per cent. (*see* Table 1.2)

In the context of Cuttack district, the rise of percentage of traditional irrigated land was possible because of the aggregate rise of irrigated land from 1939-40 to 1941-42 around 23,000 acres additionally (probably extension of agriculture took place). In 1941-

Table 1.2: Share of Traditional Irrigational Sources to the Total Irrigation sector
(*in percentage*)

Year	*Cuttack*	*Balasore*	*Puri*
1939-40	24.91	11.49	100
1941-42	29.94	11.28	100
1943-44	26.00	11.13	100
1944-45	27.95	11.72	100
1945-46	30.32	12.65	95.39

Source: Season and Crop Reports of Orissa for the Years 1939-40 to 1945-46.

42, under private canals around 4,000 acres of land additionally irrigated, whereas under other sources there was rise of around 10,000 acres additional comparing to the year 1939-40. And under tanks around 8,000 acres of land additionally irrigated. Followed by in 1943-44, though there was increase in the aggregate irrigated land by nearly 14,000, still the share of traditional water sources went down as, government canal system stood at the forefront in this year. But in the very next year traditional water sources irrigated land's share went up slightly because there was an addition of nearly 10,000 acres of land was under this kind of sources, whereas under government canal only 3,000 acres of land. In 1945-46, there was little decline in the aggregate irrigated land, but under the traditional kind of sources an addition of nearly 8,000 acres of land was irrigated whereas under government canal sector there was a decline of 10,000 acres owing to good rainfall. Similarly in the context of Balasore district, its share declined till 1943-44 as there was steady decrease in the total irrigated land. From 1944-45 it starts rising as once again the total irrigated land grew slowly. In 1945-46, its rise was little substantial as there was an addition of 1,250 acres of land was under the command of well irrigation. In Puri, only in 1945-46 the share of traditional water sources declined. This was all because of the government canals extension which stood with only 10,000 acres of land under its command.

From Table 1.2, it is very clear that, out of all the three districts,

Puri had a large number of different traditional irrigational sources; the traditional sources covered almost all the irrigational areas. The British introduced canal system did not touch to the district even till last hour of independence. Only on the eve of independence canal irrigation touched to the district. Followed by Cuttack district, which maintained second position in this regard (availability of traditional water sources), whereas Balasore remained at last. It does not mean that in Cuttack and Balasore, the traditional sources of irrigation were weak in the past. Rather there was a declination of those kinds of water sources with the advent of canal system. That is the reason why irrigation from traditional sources did not take place much both in Balasore and Cuttack district.

In the pre-colonial Coastal Orissa, in the years of good rainfall, the Oriya peasants used to cultivate their land without much taking the help of traditional sources. But in the years of low rainfall, it was only the traditional water sources used to manage irrigational activities. It is sufficient here to say by observing the percentage of traditional water sources that the share of traditional water sources went down much from a cent per cent of traditional irrigated land to only a very minimum level of irrigated land.

DECLINING OF THE TRADITIONAL IRRIGATIONAL SOURCES

According to Elizabeth Withcombe's argument in the context of colonial India, due to the extension of canal irrigation under the East India Company, thousands of tanks went disused and also disappeared in the countryside. With the introduction of canals, the water table went up and made common earthen wells unstable. However, a 1901 government estimate stated that the private works (tanks, wells, rivers, streams, and ponds) dominated only 60 per cent of the total area under irrigation.[50] And the cause of those sources existence was the availability of *takkavi* loans. Coming to the slow and steady demise of traditional sources in Orissa, there were many causes for this kind of pitiable condition.

Firstly, the high emphasis and prior to the introduction of the canal irrigation; the negligence and half-hearted or total ignorance to conventional water sources were the major causes that led to the decline of traditional water sources. The best example in order to illustrate the indifference attitude of the colonial government towards traditional water sources, which caused for the declination of substantial number of traditional water sources (particularly tanks) was in colonial Andhra region.[51] Hence, they concentrated much on the canal irrigation.

It should be remembered that prior to the introduction of the modern canal system of irrigation by the British, the peasants in Orissa were largely dependent on rainfall for cultivation and as and when the monsoon failed, they availed other traditional modes of irrigation such as tanks and streams and so on. However, when the modern form of canal system was implemented in Coastal Orissa, the peasants began to look at it as a major source of irrigation, not because they had no choice of other, as the British could convince them about the economic benefit of their project. Keeping all the evil intentions, they projected only the economic benefits of canal irrigation for the peasants, which neutralised the Orissa peasants. With the course of time, peasants in the region neglected the traditional water sources; forgot to maintain or revive them. Since the peasants were economically poor they did not maintained these traditional water sources. On the other hand, the British also did not give attention to it for its maintenance.

Secondly, the British motto was little investment and maximum profit. The British fully understood that revival of the traditional water sources did not fetch them any profit. Nor the emancipation of the peasants was not their intention. But on the other hand, construction of canals had brought multiple benefits for them. Benefit here means they had the control over the agriculture. They could also make different kinds of economic gains out of the canal, such as, navigational income, irrigational income, trade, and other commercial benefits. Those aspects haunted them mentally to initiate the canal project. The colonialists paid attention to the traditional water sources only when the canal irrigation method was not suitable to be applied in certain areas (like Gujarat) due to geographical and other such reasons. Secondly, Famine Commissions which enquired into the famine conditions in the country also insisted on the revival of the traditional water sources. Improvement of those sources was expected through the form of financial helps such as *takkavi*[52] (agricultural loans).

Thirdly, the method of contract for irrigation from canal system was also indirectly responsible for the slow demise of indigenous water sources. Peasants were enforced to go for a contract with a fixed amount of water rate. Those contracts were both long term and short term. In the case of short term contract, the water tax amount was high whereas, the price was comparably little less in the case of long term contracts.[53] Peasants never got a chance to look back into their traditional water sources: there was no space for either for the preservation or for the maintenance of it under the contract system. They were all forced to be entangled within the burden of canal system and stock to its bondage of tax. In addition to this, the heavy exaction of land tax too attributed to the demise of those water sources without a fight.

Much before the arrival of the British, the local lords were the one who always used to promote those kinds of traditional water sources with the intention to improve agriculture, which could bring them a good amount as share.[54] But in the colonial period those local lords like the *Zamindars* or landlords did not do anything for the improvement of agriculture or estates as was stated by L.S.S. O'Malley in his *Puri Gazetteers* in 1929.[55] But they did not forget to exact various forms of illegal taxes. Of course in this matter it would be enough to say that even the local lords had no real power as like earlier from every respect and it was the colonial master used to direct them to the way they want.

Initially, the slow and steady process of decline of traditional water sources was not felt by the poor peasants under the wheels of the pressure of different kinds of financial burdens. But in the long run, the decline of the traditional water sources impacted them heavily. Before the introduction of modern form of canal irrigation system peasants used to depend upon only their devised ways. Hence, the irrigation was carried cent per cent from traditional water sources. From the lastly given statistics it has been proved how a cent per cent traditional water sources irrigated land turned into a minimum user of traditional water source. Hence, the British conceived canal system is responsible in a major way for destroying the age old water sources.

IMPACT OF THE DECLINE OF TRADITIONAL IRRIGATION ON ORISSA ECONOMY

The loss of those traditional water sources brought a long term impact of the peasantry. The first significant impact was that, the indigenous concepts and practices of irrigation which was practiced over centuries had ruined drastically with the coming of canal system. There was a shift in the crop pattern from the subsistence nature; which was one of the order of those days. Food production was the main pivot of concentration through the traditional water sources. Loss of such sources brought now loss of mastery over the indigenous knowledge of traditional irrigation.

Secondly, with the loss of such traditional irrigational sources, the spirit of independency in the field of irrigation lost forever. Those traditional water sources were managed as well as maintained by the poor peasants through a community method. Everyone had the full responsibility for looking after those sources. Dependency on canal irrigation had grown completely and the peasants were forced to accept the terms and conditions of the British. They were left in the mercy hands of the white masters. That precarious situation was such unique that, as if the Orissa peasants sold their freedom to the colonialists by themselves. This is discussed further in the last chapter four in an elaborated manner.

The above arguments clearly show that Orissa had a big loss because of the loss of the traditional water sources. Before the introduction of the canal system, Orissa was independent from irrigational point of view. With the advent of canal system, many laws, regulations came into force in the agricultural sector. Orissa became a mere follower of the British regulations. Starting from water tax to navigational income and all other things were monopolised by them. Excess assessment of water tax turned Orissa's economy as weak. The net result of the British economic policy was the prevalence of extreme poverty among its people during the entire period of British rule down to 1947. The administrative reports of the period under review disclose that there prevailed extreme poverty during the period under review. Most of the income went to the colonial rulers.

During the time of scarcities Orissa region used to manage those situations with the help of those water sources in earlier days. The state had a unique position in the field of traditional irrigation pattern all-over India, as it had possessed the sense of self-dependency in the irrigation sector. With the coming of modern canal irrigation ways, the peasants were not in a position to irrigate their land according to their will, as the state had possessed very minimum number of traditional water sources in some places and in some places there were no traditional water sources.

In the next chapter the causes for the introduction of British Canal Irrigation and the extension of canal irrigation are discussed in a detailed manner.

Notes

1. Narain, A.A. (1997). *Dying Wisdom: Rise, Fall and Potential of India's Traditional Water Harvesting*, Centre for Science and Environment, New Delhi, p. 11.

2. O'Malley, L.S.S. (1933). *Bihar and Orissa District Gazetteers, Cuttack,* Government of Bihar and Orissa, p. 92. (Here onwards *BODG: Cuttack*), New Delhi: Logos Press.
3. Owen, G.E. (1922). *Bihar and Orissa in 1921,* Government of Bihar and Orissa, Patna, p. 49.
4. Mishra, Rudraprasanna (2017). "Krusi: Arthanitira Godara Goda ?" *The Samaj,* Balesore, 13 April, 2017, p. 6.
5. Sengupta, N. "Irrigation: Traditional vs Modern", *Economic and Political Weekly,* Vol. 20 (No. 45/47), 1985, November, pp. 1919-1938.
6. A.A. Narain, *op. cit.,* p. 236.
7. O'Malley, L.S.S. (1929). *Bihar and Orissa District Gazetteers, Puri,* Government of Bihar and Orissa, Logos Press, New Delhi: pp. 165-166. (Here onwards *BODG: Puri*)
8. Narain, A.A. *op. cit.,* p. 242.
9. *BODG: Puri,* p. 166.
10. Narain, A.A., *op. cit.,* p. 242.
11. *Ibid.*
12. *BODG: Cuttack,* pp. 79-80.
13. Narain, A.A. *op. cit.,* p. 242.
14. *BODG: Cuttack,* pp. 79-80.
15. Narain, A.A. *op. cit.,* p. 242.
16. Pradhan, Nagendranath (2010). *Gangadhar Granthavali, Krushak Samgita, Krushakara Atmakatha* (Odia book), Dharmagrantha Store, Cuttack, new edition p. 360.
17. Narain, A.A. *op. cit.,* p. 236.
18. *BODG: Puri,* p. 166.
19. Maddox, S.L. (1990). *Final Report on the Survey and Settlement of the Province of Orissa, 1890-1900,* Vol. I, Government of Bengal, Calcutta, p. 98.
20. *BODG: Cuttack,* p. 79 and S.L. Maddox, *op. cit.,* p. 98.
21. *Ibid., Puri,* p. 166.
22. Maddox, S.L. *op. cit.,* p. 98.
23. *BODG: Cuttack,* p. 79.
24. *The Famine Inquiry Commission, Final Report,* Government of India, Madras, Delhi, 1945, p. 134.
25. *BODG: Cuttack,* p. 79.
26. *Ibid., Puri,* p. 166.
27. *The Famine Inquiry Commission, Final Report, op. cit.,* p. 135.

28. *BODG: Puri*, p. 166.
29. *Ibid., Cuttack*, p. 80; *BODG: Puri*, p. 167.
30. *Ibid., Puri*, p. 167; *BODG: Cuttack*, p. 80 and S.L. Maddox, *op. cit.*, p. 98.
31. *Ibid., Puri*, p. 167.
32. *BODG: Cuttack*, p. 80 and S.L. Maddox, *op. cit.*, p. 98.
33. *Ibid., Puri*, p. 167 and *BODG: Cuttack*, p. 80.
34. Maddox, S.L. *op. cit.*, p. 98.
35. *Season and Crop Report of Orissa for the year 1939-40*, Government of Orissa, Cuttack, 1941, p. 10 (Here onwards *SCRO*) and *Agricultural Statistics of Orissa for 1939-40*, Government of Orissa, Cuttack, 1943, p. 1.
36. *SCRO, 1941-42*, p. 6.
37. *Ibid., 1943-44*, p. 6.
38. *Ibid., 1944-45*, p. 6.
39. *Ibid., 1945-46*, p. 6.
40. *Ibid., 1939-40*, p. 10 and *Agricultural Statistics of Orissa for 1939-40*, p. 1.
41. *Ibid., 1941-42*, p. 6.
42. *Ibid., 1943-44*, p. 6.
43. *Ibid., 1944-45*, p. 6.
44. *Ibid., 1945-46*, p. 6.
45. *Ibid., 1939-40*, p. 10; and *Agricultural Statistics of Orissa for 1939-40*, p. 1.
46. *Ibid., 1941-42*, p. 6.
47. *Ibid., 1943-44*, p. 6.
48. *Ibid., 1944-45*, p. 6.
49. *Ibid., 1945*-46, p. 6.
50. Whitcombe, E. (1984). "Irrigation", In: D. Kumar and M. Desai (Ed.), *The Cambridge Economic History of India* (Vol. II), New Delhi: Orient Longman Private Limited, pp. 677-737.
51. Vijay Kumar, T. (2015). "Irrigation Politics and the Anicuts in Andhra", in Adapa Satyanarayan, (Ed.), *Early Modern Andhra Hyderabad and Company Rule AD 1724-1857*, Emesco Books, Hyderabad, pp. 132-145.
52. *Report of the Indian Famine Commission, 1901 and Papers Relating Thereto*, Darling Son Ltd., London, 1901, pp. 102-103.

53. *Report of the Irrigation Rates Revision Committee*, Government of Orissa, 1967, p. 13.
54. See for instance Sohini Sengupta, *op. cit.*
55. Bhola, S.C. (1990). *British Economic Policy in Orissa (1905-1947)*, New Delhi: Discovery Publishing House, pp. 141-144.

2
Introduction of the Canal Irrigation and its Extension

> If railway construction will be there, not even the constructed cost will come back. Hence, canals are more suitable for Orissa than railway.
>
> —*A General Administration Report on Orissa Division: 1872-1873*[1]

REASONS FOR THE INTRODUCTION OF CANAL IRRIGATION IN COASTAL ORISSA

Not even a single step was taken by the colonial rulers without any ulterior motive. The construction of canals in Orissa was not an exception to this. It was one of those typical attempts by the British to project themselves as the rightful masters who placed the welfare of their subjects before anything. In other words, keeping many objectives behind the canal construction, the British tried to project themselves as a welfare government.[2] It is true that the great famine of Orissa in 1866 did influence such an enormous decision to go ahead with the construction of the canal in the state. However, most prominent factors behind the decision were the scope for making profit by different ways such as taxation way and trade and commerce. However, the imperialist historians did not want to write about them.[3] But there are historical records available to prove the evil intentions behind whole canal irrigation project. This chapter will discuss about its reasons behind the project in detail and the whole course of canal construction over different periods.

Explicit Causes

Orissa with a long coast was subjected to natural calamities often. Drought too played a havoc inviting intermittent famine. The devastation created by the natural calamities brought the attention of the British Government and that became one of the reasons behind the introduction of the new irrigation system.[4] The immediate provocation was the severe famine of 1866 that forced the government to look into the large scale destruction. An investigation committee was set up to look into the matter under Sir George Campbell. It found that the lack of irrigation facilities led to the situation along with other causes.[5] The committee suggested that the Government should explore the possibilities of construction of a canal system to mitigate the situation.[6] The consecutive scarcities in Puri district in 1877-78, 1885-86, 1888-89, 1897, 1908, and 1918-20[7], and in Cuttack and Balasore districts incurred over many years. 1877-78, 1897, and 1901 famines touched every district and devastated the economy as a whole. Puri district witnessed droughts for longer duration as the monsoon failed repeatedly. It affected the paddy cultivation, the subsistence crop, adversely; in some places the crop failed entirely and other places the harvest was too poor. It took place in the case of mostly winter rice, while it was the mainstay of Orissa people.[8] Similarly, floods were yet other natural calamities that played havoc in the coastal Orissa; that too to be contained. In other words the British had to take adequate measurers to check the heavy devastation of frequently occurred floods too.[9] The proposed canal irrigation project was influenced by these above said factors.

It should be noted here that Famine Commission of the Indian Government of 1898 recommended the construction of irrigation canal in Orissa and the Government took over the charge of it soon.

The Indian Famine Commission of 1901, however, emphasized on the necessity of both the canal and traditional irrigation systems for the betterment of agricultural production in the State and thus address the famine situation effectively.[10] Its recommendations were insightful than the first commission. However, there were other decisive factors which finally led to the construction of irrigation canals in Orissa, these factors will be discussed in the following sections.

Economic Factors

Ian Stone argued that the main motive of the British to introduce canal irrigation system was to control the people and land of India. He said that the introduction of such canal systems was the last attempt to subdue the local people politically without much effort.[11] It is a fact that, from the day one of their arrival, the British followed a policy of political aggrandisement. One after another they devised steps to subjugate the people of the country whether it was through subsidiary alliance or doctrine of lapse or many such other measurers. Their intervention in the agrarian sector changed the landownership pattern and the existing land relations. The new land revenue and taxation introduced by the British put the burden on the poor and middle peasants.[12] The canal irrigation system was yet another tool the British used to subjugate the peasantry completely.

The economic motive was the major factor behind the project. Constructing such irrigational projects was necessary to the British in expanding the commercial crops in various places of India. And this irrigation system would assure them a good return of lavish revenue in different ways like water tax and land tax. Since many canals were also used for the navigation, they also got navigational income. Along with that they also anticipated for the stability of revenue accumulation and the enhancement of taxing capacity.[13] Side by side, the expectation for profit out of internal as well as external trade ignited them in introducing the system.[14] But most of the master records indicate that it was basically intended for the navigation and modern form of irrigation.[15]

Transport and communication between Calcutta and Cuttack was a major concern of the British. The desire to improve the communication channels – which was basic and very poor— also played role in the construction of the canal. The road that connected Cuttack and Calcutta was very unsafe due to high incidence of dacoits. The road was also very bad. Hence, the transportation of various goods was much time consuming.[16] Canal was devoid of all these problems. The whole of Orissa canal system was devised to connect Cuttack with Calcutta along with other intentions.[17]

There is also another view regarding the construction of canals. As Orissa did not have good road and transport connections, reaching food to the people during the time of the great famine of 1866, became too difficult a task, hence the British concentrated much on this aspect.[18]

It was also the outlook of the British officials who were there for sometimes, that Orissa's main economy was dependent on agriculture. Along with that it had very good river system. Fertile land used to produce very good amount of food crops. Hence, the British clearly understood that without much investment they could easily access a lavish amount of return through different ways as said earlier, such as water tax, land tax, and navigational charges. It will also empower them to colonize agriculture of Orissa.

Yet another factor was that Orissa state had abundant labour; cheap labour was available for every kind of work. As per the official records, it was the intention of the British behind the various construction works to give employment to the labour class.[19] In fact, the colonial rulers wanted to use the cheap labour available in the region for constructing the canals for their future revenues.

Canal Construction in Orissa

Profit was always the priority of the British Raj as the East India

Company. Wherever the possibility of profit was less the British did not go for that.[20] Orissa canal system project was not an exception to this. This is evident in a statement of an officer in the *General Administration Report on Orissa Division: 1872-1873*; while exploring the benefit of the construction of the canals in Orissa to the British Government it said, "If railway construction will be there, not even the constructed cost will come back. Hence canals are more suitable for Orissa than railway."[21]

With all these above reasons, the British Government began the construction of many canals in Orissa. The canals which were used for irrigation as well as navigation purposes were (a) the Kendrapara Canal, with its extension to Jambu and two branches called the Gobri and Patamundai canals; besides, these canals, another canal called the Gobri extension canal, which drew water from the Kendrapara canal by means of the Patamundai canal; (b) the High Level Canal; (c) the Taladanda canal, with its branch canal the Machgaon canal[22]; (d) the Orissa Coast Canal[23]; (e) the Jajpur Canal, and (f) the Dudhai Canal.[24] The canal system which was constructed in Cuttack and Balasore districts was broadly known as the Orissa Canals.[25] The land between the main stream of the Mahanadi and the Brahmani was irrigated by the Patamundai canal on the north, and the Kendrapara canal on the south, the Gobri canal formed a connecting link between them to the east. Both these systems drew their supply of water from the south flank of the anicut across the Birupa, which also feeds the High Level canal. The anicut of the Mahanadi used to feed the Taladanda and Machgaon canals.[26]

Now, let us look at the process of the construction of canals in the coastal districts of colonial Orissa.

The unprecedented and devastating flood of 1855 was the immediate provocation for the British government to moot the idea. Captain Harris, the responsible officer, strategized the effective effluence of the surplus water of the rivers in Orissa by constructing channels from a storage point to save the country from inundation.[27] The initial proposal to employ the rivers of Orissa in the field of irrigation came from General Sir Arthur Cotton of Madras Engineers.[28] He was sent to Orissa for a visit in 1858 for a feasibility study of the project and to give suggestions for controlling flood waters of the River Mahanadi. It was he who proposed to carry out the works of canal irrigation work, similar to the works that were taken in the deltas of the Godavari and Krishna in order to check the frequent occurrences of flood.[29] Sir Cotton specifically attached the importance of navigation for such a project along with irrigation facilities. He estimated that the system will have the capacity to irrigate an area of 22.50 lakhs of acres and navigation would be opened up between Orissa, Midnapur and Calcutta. According to him, the project was to cost about $ 13,00,000.[30]

In 1860, a joint stock company on the name of the East India Irrigation and Canal Company (E.I.I.C.C.) was formed for the purpose of carrying out the canal works in Orissa.[31] The work of the construction of irrigation and navigation canals was entrusted under a contract in 1862 to it. The anicuts (a dam made in the course of a stream for the purpose of regulating the flow of a system of irrigation) at Jobra and Naraj were commenced in 1863 and water was first supplied for irrigation in 1865 in Cuttack.[32] In 1866, a devastating famine visited Orissa. Initially the Orissa canal project began by the East India Irrigation and Canal Company (E.I.I.C.C.) from 1868.[33] When the company found it difficult to raise fund, as the company lost the hope of recovery because of the great famine, the Government of India purchased the whole of the works for the sum of Rs. 109 lakhs in 1869.[34] In the course of time, the government took over the Orissa canals from the East Indian Irrigation Canal Company towards the end of the ninteenth century showing some kind of difficulties.[35] But there is also other view on the existence of the Company. After the purchase of all the works of E.I.I.C.C. by the Government of India, the Company ceased to exist by 1869.[36] The initial estimated cost for the Orissa canal project was Rs. 3,23,15,845.[37] The original plan of the project was greatly modified and the plan for construction of canals in Puri and Balasore districts was abandoned later.

Ultimately, three canal systems were sanctioned, namely, Taladanda and Machgaon Canals serving the Mahanadi-Kathjori Doab, Pattamundai and Kendrapara Canals with Jambu and Gobri extension to serve the Mahanadi-Birupa Doab and the High Level Canals to serve the lands at the foothills from Cuttack to Bhadrak.[38]

The Kendrapara Canal

It was the oldest (opened in 1869) and the most important canals in Orissa.[39] It starts from the River Birupa at Jagatpur, just above the anicut, skirts the northern bank of the Mahanadi and its tributary River Nuana for a distance of 39 miles. It used to irrigate the area between the Mahanadi and the Gobri drainage channel. It had the discharge capacity of 1,067 cubic feet per second. By 1900 it had 23 distributaries, which used to cover an area of a vast stretched land.[40] It used to irrigate the land between the Mahanadi and the Gobri drainage channel. It was originally constructed to advance the transport and communication between Cuttack and False Point harbour.[41]

By 1872-73, the *Kendrapara* Canal (started in 1869) had already connected with Cuttack and it was expected to connect up to the False Point.[42] But in the following year expansion was in slow process because of adequate rainfall.[43] The Kendrapara canal's work was completed till Marsaghai by July 1876.[44] By the year 1912-1913, two distributary works on the Kendrapara Canal were completed.[45]

The Gobri Canal

This canal is a branch canal of the Kendrapara canal, taking off from the 32nd mile and it runs 15 miles (total length) towards east to the Gundakia River. It was originally intended to be a distributary canal, but afterwards made a navigable one in order to facilitate communication between Cuttack and Chanbali.[46] Then it became the best possible route from Cuttack to Chanbali. It used to cover *parganas* like Tikan, Derabisi, and Chhedra. However, as far as the irrigational facilities were concerned, it had the very limited discharge capacity of 373 cubic feet per second.[47]

By July 1876, the construction works of this canal was half finished.[48] By 1912-13, a permanent outlet was completed. In the same year the distributary work of the canal Gobri was completed about half by this time. And some extent extension work on the Gobri (main canal) was going on.[49] During the year 1915-16 some minor tributary works were over on this canal.[50]

The Patamundai Canal

This canal was a branch canal of the Kendrapara Canal. This canal left the Kendrapara Canal just below the head works at Jagatpur and skirts the southern bank of the river Birupa down to Indipur, where it begins to turn southward, and falls into the Gobri Extension near Albha after a circuit house course of 47 miles. It was not a navigable canal. It used to command over few highly rich areas like, Sungara, Matkatnagar, and Chaudakulat.[51] It had discharging capacity of 885 cubic feet per second.[52]

This canal was extended from the Kendrapara canal form 1872-73.[53] By next year the process of construction became very slow. But during 1874-75 expansion was in slow process because of adequate rainfall.[54] By July 1876, it was half finished.[55] Even during 1906-07. the extension work of the Pattamundai canal's distributary was still in continuation.[56] By 1912-13, a permanent outlet was finished. And the distributary work of Pattamundai was completed about half by this time. In the same year it was seen that, some extension work on the Pattamundai Canal (main canal) was going on.[57] This even continued in 1915-17.[58]

The Gobri Extension Canal

The canal was a short one, only 6 miles long and formed as a connecting link between river Gandakia and the river Brahmani at Albha. It used to draw its water partly from the Patamundai Canal and partly from the rivers and used to irrigate the *pargana* of Utikan. It had the capacity to discharge 648 cubic feet water per second. It was an important canal for navigation purpose also.[59]

The High Level Canal

It was designed to provide a navigable trade route between Cuttack and Calcutta, and also to irrigate the country. It had three ranges. The construction work of Range I started from 1869-70 and in the same year it started working.[60] The Range I started from river Birupa and connected to the river Brahmani, a distance of 33 miles and Range II starts from the Brahmani to the Baitarani river, a distance of 12½ miles. The III Range was about 39 miles. It went through Cuttack and Balasore districts.[61] The work of Range II and Range III started in 1879-80.[62]

The High level canal was intended to connect with the Midnapore canal during 1872-73.[63] By 1874, the High level canal opened to the River Brahmani and excavation work was completed up to the River Salundee.[64] But during 1874-75 expansion was in slow process because of adequate rainfall.[65] During 1877-78, for the first time the third range of the High level canal was extended in Balasore district.[66] The extension work of the third range was still incomplete by July 1879.[67] The High Level Canal was extended to Bhadrak. This canal helped Orissa people (the colonialist's claim that the canal helped Orissa people) to have better transport and communication between Cuttack and Bhadrak.[68] Irrigation facility was available for (mainly) the southern part of Balasore district, roughly 20 miles of the High Level Canal by 1884.[69] By 1884-85, the third Range of the High Level Canal went only 18 miles through Bhadrak sub-division irrigating only 2872 acres of land.[70]

By the year 1912-1913, one minor distributary work on the High Level Canal was completed. Along with that some extension works of two distributaries on the High Level Canal were still in continuation.[71] Even this continued till 1915-16.[72]

The Taladanda Canal

The construction of Taladanda Canal work started in the period 1870-71.[73] The Taladanda canal starts from the right bank of the river Mahanadi at Jobra and runs towards south-east direction to Fakirpara where it confluence the Machgaon branch. From there it skirts the southern bank of the river Sukpaika to Jajpur, and from Jajpur to Taladanda it flows the course of river Mahanadi. It had the discharge capacity of 1342 cubic feet per second. It used to cover over a huge area that includes Kodinda, Hariharpur, Jhankar, Tiran, and Kandhi.[74] It was designed for the purpose of irrigating the triangular tract of the state between the Mahanadi and Katjuri.[75] Along with that the canal was constructed generally with the prime aim of transport and communication.[76]

The construction work of the canal was in continuation in very slow manner during 1873-74.[77] But again during 1874-75 expansion was in slow process because of adequate rainfall.[78] The Taladanda canal was still unfinished by July 1876. It was expected to connect the canal with Paradeep, which would help them for navigation. Though it was mainly constructed for navigation still it used to command a vast stretch of land for irrigation.[79] The Taladanda Extension Canal work met its completion by 1894-95.[80] By the year 1912-1913, one distributary work was completed on the Taladanda Canal. During that year the extension work of one minor distributary on the Taladanda Canal was in progress.[81]

The Machgaon Canal

It is a branch canal of the Taladanda Canal. The canal starts at the Taladanda canal (Birbati square) 7 miles south of Cuttack, and runs along the north bank of the Katjuri and of its Branch Alanka. It had a discharging capacity of 776 cubic feet per second. It was originally intended to extend this canal as far as Machgaon so as to run into the tidal water of the Devi River, and thus establish connection with the sea, but the scheme was not carried out. It stopped at 6 miles short of Machgaon.[82]

The construction works of the *Machgaon* canal was going on during 1872-73.[83] Even during 1873-74, the construction work was going on, but in very slow manner.[84] The canal was constructed generally with the prime aim of transport and communication. But in the very next year expansion was in slow process because of adequate rainfall.[85] The construction works of this canal finished up to Chatro by July 1876 and was intended to extend up to Machgaon.[86] In order to prevent drought, the authorities felt the importance of the extension of the Machgaon Canal.[87] By the year 1912-1913, two minor distributary works on the Machgaon Canal were completed. By the same year the extension work of one distributary on the Machgaon Canal was in continuation.[88]

The Coast Canal

The construction work of the canal started in 1880-81. It mostly designed not to yield profit but to get protection from famine by improving communication between Orissa and Calcutta. Side by side it was expected as a remunerative one. The canal connected the Hoogly at Geonkhali with the river Matai at Charbatia near Bhadrak. Within Orissa only its length was 92 miles. It had four ranges. Its Range III connected the river Rasulpur in Hidgelle with the river Subarnarekha of Balasore district, with total length of 31¼ miles; Range IVA the river Subarnarekha with the river Panchapara, total length of 17 miles; Range IV B connected to the river Panchapara with Burabalanga river, a length of seven miles and Range V connected the river Burabalanga with the river Matai of Bhadrak.[89] Construction work was going on in full swing by 1882-83.[90] Ranges IVA and V were temporarily opened for traffic from 15th July to 31st December,

1886. For the first time (full 92 miles) it was completely opened on 1st September, 1887. With the opening of railway in Orissa its use came down. The canal was fed by tidal water. Hence, it was no more useful for the people from irrigation point of view. On the other hand, the high level expectation of the colonialists did not meet its point of success. The Flood Advisory Committee of 1928 proposed for the abandonment of the canal for which the Ranges IV -A and IV-B of the canal were abandoned.[91]

The Jajpur Canal

It was the youngest canal out of the total canal system in Orissa. Its construction work started in 1890-91 and it started irrigating land in 1891-92.[92] It originates from the point of bifurcation of the Burah and Baitarani rivers, runs 6½ miles in an easterly direction up to Jajpur town. It was a navigable one. And further it had the discharge capacity of 700 cubic feet per second.[93] However, another official document contests this and states that it had the capacity of 600 cubic feet per second only.[94]

A large amount of distributary work of the Jajpur Canal was done during 1894-95.[95] This happened because of two preceding years' low rainfall.[96] By the year 1912-1913, extension work of one minor distributary on the Jajpur Canal was in progress.[97] Some minor distributary works were over by 1915-16.[98]

The Dudhai Canal

It was a channel in the name of the Dudhai Canal. It started from the Brahmani weir. It had been completed for 36 miles out of the sanctioned length of 46 miles. It was intended to irrigate about 12,000 acres of land in the area between the river Brahmani and the river Kharsua. But this channel had proved failure and had been abandoned in 1930.[99]

From the above narrative it is obvious claim that with the

intention of maximizing revenue, the British started canal construction. Flood and rainfall always mattered for the progress of the construction of canal. After 1897-98, the process became little slow. All the canals confided only to Balasore and Cuttack district whereas, Puri was out of the canal system.

EXTENSION OF VARIOUS CANALS

By 1884 the total lengths of different canals were as follows:

Table 2.1: Lengths of Different Canals by 1884

Canal name	*Length (in miles)*
Kendrapara and Gobri	54
High Level	64
Kendrapara Extension	15
Taladanda	27
Machgaon	19
Patamoondi	47
Total	**226**

Source: *Annual General Report*, Orissa Division, for 1883-84, Cuttack, 1884, p. 36.

By 1890-91, there were total 177 miles of canal for irrigation and navigation and 75 miles are only for irrigation.[100] By the year 1915-1916, the total length of Orissa main canals was 223¾ miles, total branch canals was 103 miles.[101] But the total length of main canals and branch canals showed no change till 1917-18.[102] In 1919-20 year, the total lengths of main canal showed little change. Including a little addition the total length reached to 224¼ miles which was stagnant from 1915-1916.[103] During 1920-1921, no important work was undertaken due to unusual floods in August 1920. Attention was paid only on maintenance.[104] All the nine canals in Orissa circle were closed for an aggregate of 448 days for repairs.[105] However, by

1922, the total length of Orissa Canals including both main and branch canals was 327½ miles of which the total navigable canal was 205½ miles.[106] Under Orissa coast canal the length of both main and branch canals for navigation only was 95½ miles.[107] Around 1927-28, it was seen that the Orissa canal system scarcely pay their working expenses.[108] It seems, the process of canal extension was stagnant. Followed by the next year 1929-30, there was no extra addition in the process of canal extension due to normal and satisfactory rainfall.[109] However, the Orissa canal system included 268 miles of main canals by 1932.[110] On the other hand, 199 miles of main canal was opened for irrigation and navigation whereas 75 miles of main canal was specifically devoted for irrigation by the end of financial year 1938-39.[111] The process of canal construction activity in 1930s was very slow. The total trend of canal construction was:

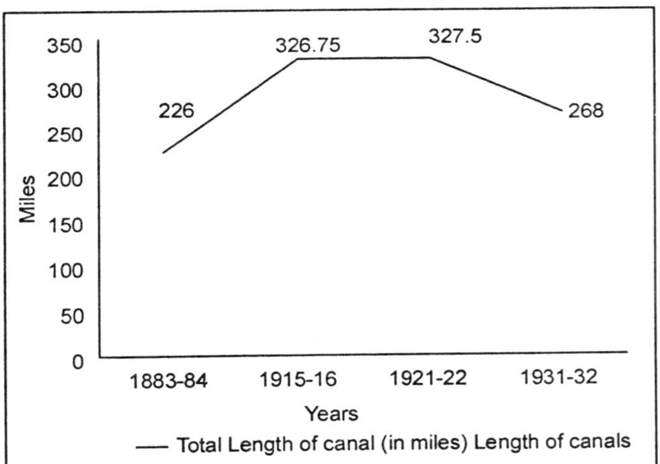

Fig. 2.1: Total Lengths of Canals (in miles).

Source: *Annual General Report, Orissa Division, for 1883-84*, Cuttack, 1884, p. 36; *RABO*, 1915-1916, p. 67; *Bihar and Orissa First Decennial Review, 1912-1922*, Government of Bihar and Orissa, Patna, 1923, p. 2; *BODG: Cuttack*, p. 105.

Till 1921-22, the extension of canals continued. But only after ten years interval the total lengths of the canal came down to some extent. It was so because of the abandonment of Range IV-A and Range IV-B of the Coast Canal in 1928 which were about 24 miles[112] and the complete abandonment of Dudhai Canal in November 1930, which was about 36 miles.[113] But after 1940, the construction works stopped owing to the beginning of the Second World War, which was evident indirectly from the amount kept for the canal irrigated area during the 1940s as there was no substantial increase.

Most of the canals profited much to Cuttack and Balasore district. In Puri there was no regular irrigation works. For the first time, attention was paid on the irrigation facilities of Puri district with the help of the Khas Mahal Improvement Fund from 1885-86.[114] Also some minor irrigation works were executed from Estates Improvement Fund.[115] Later on, the irrigation development programme was broadened and the finance came from three sources— the Miscellaneous Improvement Fund, Khas Mahal Fund and Agricultural Improvement Fund from 1887-88.[116] Only towards the independence of India, Puri district was connected with canals, which can be seen from the *Season and Crop Report* that it irrigated around 10,000 acres of land in 1945-46.[117]

Construction of Distributary Canals

By 1890-91, there were 764¾ miles of distributaries and village channels.[118] The extension works of some minor distributaries were still going on during the year 1906-1907.[119] During 1907-1908, several minor distributaries were constructed. In order to prevent drought, the authorities felt the importance of the extension of the Machgaon Canal. The Balasore flood of 1906-1907 compelled the government to think of other plans. For which a new proposal of the construction of irrigation canal from Baitarani and Anandapur through Agarpara across the River Salandi to River Kansbans. Similarly, construction of a canal from Bhadrak to Salandi with sluice gates at its junction was also proposed along with a channel from Salandi to Mutrigarh through Hiraghai and Khria Bundh to Duppa.[120] The Public Works Department was thinking of a scheme for the extensive irrigation works in Puri district.[121] The extension works in Cuttack was still in continuation till 1908-1909.[122]

By the year 1912-13, nearly 20.29 miles of distributaries and minor channels were added chiefly on the Taladanada, Machgaon and Kendrapara Canals.[123] By 1915-16 total distributaries were 1,287 miles against of 13 miles less in 1914-15. The total length of the total distributary included 13 miles additional distributary during the year 1915-16.[124] As for the distributaries, owing to the reasonable rainfall, the total distributaries went up to 1292 miles during 1917-18, whereas it was 1,291 in 1916-17. During the year 1917-18 there was only an addition of 5/8th mile of minor distributaries.[125] During 1918-19, the total length reached to 1,293 miles, which included an addition of 2 miles of distributaries.[126] Simultaneously, the construction of a minor distributary at Solanpur was going on from the High Level Canal Range III during that year.[127] The earth work of that distributary was about to complete. The next year in 1919-1920, only over a mile of distributary was added.[128] Including the additional one the total length of distributary reached to 1,294 miles against the last year length 1,293 miles.[129] By 1922, the total length of distributary channels was 1295½ miles.[130] By 1932, there were 1,300 miles of distributaries including minor or village channels.[131] But, the total length of distributaries reached to only 1302 miles by 1938-39.[132] (*see* Fig 2.2)

The length of distributaries went up. Fig. 2.2 clearly shows that there was continuous progress of distributaries. But after 1931-32, the process of progress was very slow as it is shown in Fig. 2.2. Already by 1931-32 the construction works of main canals were stopped but distributary works continued. Then after the process of progress must have slow, as it was already the time of freedom movement and British did not concentrate much on the aspect which has been proved in the next chapter as there was not much progress of canal irrigation.

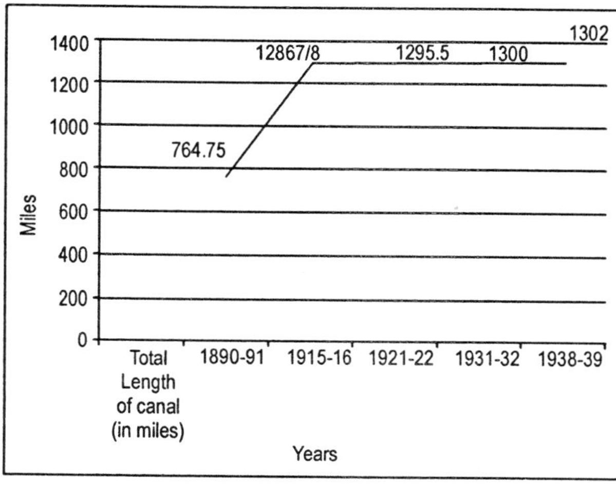

Fig. 2.2: Total Lengths of Distributaries (in miles).

Source: *Report on the Administration of Bengal, 1890-91*. p. 24; *RABO*, 1915-1916, p. 67; *Bihar and Orissa First Decennial Review*, 1912-1922, Government of Bihar and Orissa, Patna, 1923, p. 2; *BODG: Cuttack*, p. 105; Jadu Nath Mahapatra, Orissa in 1936-37 to 1938-39, Government of Orissa, Cuttack, 1941, p. 131.

To conclude, the colonialists claimed that due to the famines and frequent occurrences of floods they took the initiative to introduce canal system in Orissa in order to protect the land. But keeping the motive of economic profit behind the canal construction project they went ahead in their desired objectives and materialised their project to which people of Orissa did not understand. Slowly and steadily the construction work was carried by them. Nine major canals were constructed all-over Coastal districts of colonial Orissa. The whole Orissa canal system was claimed by them both as productive and protective one. On the way of the progress of canal works floods and sometimes heavy rainfall obstructed to the colonialists. But on the other hand owing to dry season or short rainfall people of Orissa gave their consent for canal water. But during the good rainfall year, the poor people of Orissa did not go for the canal water, which sometimes gave them loss as it was claimed by the colonialists. As a result of that they abandoned the construction of new canals or fresh enlargement of existing canals.

Notes

1. *General Administration Report, Orissa Division for 1872-1873*, Cuttack, 1873, p. 32. (Here onwards *GAROD*)
2. For instance see, W.J. Macpherson (1972). *Economic Development in India under the British Crown, 1858-1947,* in A.J. Youngson (Ed.), *Economic Developments in the Long Run,* Routledge, London.
3. For instance see, Vera Anstey (1931). *The Economic Development of India,* London: Longmans, Green and Co. (second edition).
4. Stone, Ian (1984). *Canal Irrigation in British India: Perspectives on Technological Change in a Peasant Economy.* London: Cambridge University Press, p. 9.
5. Mishra, D.B., *op. cit.*, p. 134; Harihar Panda, *op. cit.*, p. 261; Ganeswar Nayak, "The Coast Canal in Orissa During the Colonial Era", *Orissa Review,* May-June, 2010, p. 66.
6. Grover, B.L. and S. Grover (2008). *A New Look at Modern Indian History,* New Delhi: S. Chand & Company Ltd., p. 356.
7. *BODG: Cuttack,* p. 184.
8. *Ibid.*
9. *BODG: Cuttack,* p. 100 and Jadu Nath Mahapatra, *op. cit.*, p. 131.
10. *Report of the Indian Famine Commission,* 1901, *op. cit.*, pp. 111-12.
11. Stone, Ian, *op. cit.*, 1984, p. 9.
12. Guha, Ranajit (1982). *A Rule of Property for Bengal: An Essay on the Idea of Permanent Settlement,* New Delhi: Orient Longman, 1982; Nilmani Mukherjee, *Ryotwari System in Madras 1792 1827,* Calcutta: K.L. Mukhopadhyay, 1962; Amiya Kumar Bagchi, "Land Tax, Property Rights and Peasant Insecurity in Colonial India", *The Journal of Peasant Studies,* Vol. 20, No. 1, October 1992, pp. 1-49; Eric Stokes, *English Utilitarians and India,* Delhi: Oxford University Press, 1992; Bipan Chandra, "Reinterpretation of Nineteenth Century Indian Economic History", *IESHR,* 5 (1) March 1968, reprinted in Bipan Chandra, *Nationalism and Colonialism in Modern India,* New Delhi: Orient Longman, 1987.

13. Stone, Ian, *op. cit.*, 1984, p. 9.
14. *GAROD, 1874-1875*, p. 8.
15. *Report on the Administration of Bengal, 1910-1911*, Government of Bengal, Calcutta, 1912, p. XX. Report on the Administration of Bihar and Orissa, *1917-1918*, Government of Bihar and Orissa, Patna, 1919, p. 74 (Hereafter *RABO*); *BODG: Cuttack*, p. 100.
16. Mishra, D.B., *op. cit.*, p. 134.
17. Owen, G.E. (1922). *Bihar and Orissa in 1921*, Government of Bihar and Orissa, Patna, p. 64, *BODG: Cuttack*, p. 100, Jadu Nath Mahapatra, *op. cit.*, p. 131.
18. *The Samaj*, 14th November, 2016, p. 9.
19. *Report on the Land Revenue Administration of the Lower Provinces for the 1907-1908*, Government of Bengal, Calcutta, 1908, p. 17.
20. See for example M.A. Reddy, *op. cit.*
21. *GAROD, 1872-1873*, p. 32.
22. *BODG: Cuttack*, p. 107.
23. Ganeswar Nayak, *op. cit.*, p. 66.
24. *BODG: Cuttack*, p. 107.
25. *Report of the Irrigation Rates Revision Committee, op. cit.*, p. 6.
26. *BODG: Cuttack*. p. 107.
27. *Report of the Irrigation Rates Revision Committee, op. cit.*, pp. 6-7.
28. He was responsible for the construction of Coleroon (Cauveri) anicut in Tanjore District of Madras Presidency and later he was also responsible for the construction of Godavari (in 1853) and Kistna (in 1855) anicuts, See T. Vijay Kumar, "Irrigation Politics", *op. cit.* and "Canal Irrigation under Godavari and Kistna Anicuts during Second Half of 19th Century: Certain Disadvantages", *Itihas*, Vol. XXIII, Nos. 1 & 2, 1998, pp. 115-24; D.R. Gadgil, *The Industrial Evolution in India in the Recent Times*, Oxford University Press, Delhi, 1972.
29. *BODG: Cuttack*, p. 104.
30. *Report of the Irrigation Rates Revision Committee, op. cit.*, p. 7.
31. *BODG: Cuttack*, p. 104.
32. *Report of the Irrigation Rates Revision Committee, op. cit.*, p. 7.
33. Owen, G.E., *op. cit.*,
34. *Report of the Irrigation Rates Revision Committee, op. cit.*, p. 7; *BODG: Cuttack*, p. 104.
35. Owen, G.E., *op. cit.*,
36. *BODG: Cuttack*, p. 104.

37. Maddox, S.L. (1900). *Final Report on the Survey and Settlement of the Province of Orissa, 1890-1900*, Vol. 1, Calcutta: Bengal Secretariat Press, p. 75.
38. *Report of the Irrigation Rates Revision Committee, op. cit.*, p. 7.
39. Samal, J.K. (1990). *Economic History of Orissa (1866-1912)*, New Delhi: Mittal Publications, p. 166.
40. Maddox, S.L. *op. cit.*, p. 23.
41. *BODG: Cuttack*, pp. 108-109.
42. *GAROD, 1872-1873*, p. 32.
43. *GAROD, 1874-1875*, p. 8.
44. *GAROD, 1875-1876*, p. 16.
45. *RABO, 1912-1913*, p. 71.
46. *BODG: Cuttack*, pp. 108-109.
47. Maddox, S.L., *op, cit.*, p. 23.
48. *GAROD, 1875-1876*, p. 16.
49. *RABO, 1912-1913*, p. 71.
50. *Ibid., 1915-1916*, p. 69.
51. Maddox, S.L., *op. cit.*, p. 23.
52. *BODG: Cuttack*, p. 109.
53. *GAROD, 1872-1873*, p. 32.
54. *Ibid., 1874-1875*, p. 8.
55. *Ibid., 1875-1876*, p. 16.
56. *Report of the Land Revenue Administration of the Lower Provinces for the year 1906-1907*, Government of Bengal, Calcutta, 1907, p. 18.
57. *RABO, 1912-1913*, p. 71.
58. *Ibid., 1915-1916*, p. 69.
59. Maddox, S.L., *op. cit.*, p. 23.
60. Samal, J.K., *op. cit.*, p. 166.
61. *BODG: Cuttack*, pp. 108-109.
62. Samal, J.K., *op. cit.*, p. 167.
63. *GAROD, 1872-1873*, p. 32.
64. *Ibid., 1873-1874*, p. 14.
65. *Ibid., 1874-1875*, p. 8.
66. *Annual General Administration Report, Orissa Division for 1877-78*, Cuttack, 1878, p. 30. (Here onwards *AGROD*)
67. *AGROD, 1878-79*, p. 39.
68. *Ibid., 1882-83*, p. 56.
69. *Ibid., 1883-84*, p. 36.

70. *Ibid., 1884-85*, pp. 41-42.
71. *RABO, 1912-1913*, p. 71.
72. *Ibid., 1915-1916*, p. 69.
73. *GAROD, 1873-1874*, p. 14; J.K. Samal, *op. cit.*, p. 166.
74. Maddox, S.L., *op. cit.*, p. 23.
75. *BODG: Cuttack*, p. 109.
76. *GAROD, 1874-1875*, p. 8.
77. *Ibid., 1873-1874*, p. 14.
78. *Ibid., 1874-1875*, p. 8.
79. *GAROD, 1875-1876*, p. 16.
80. *AGAROD, 1894-95*, p. 49.
81. *RABO, 1912-1913*, p. 71.
82. *Ibid.* p. 110.
83. *GAROD, 1872-1873*, p. 32.
84. *Ibid., 1873-1874*, p. 14.
85. *Ibid., 1874-1875*, p. 8.
86. *Ibid., 1875-1876*, p. 16.
87. *Report on the Land Revenue Administration of the Lower Provinces for the year 1907-1908*, Government of Bengal, Calcutta, 1908, p. 17.
88. *RABO, 1912-1913*, p. 71.
89. Nayak, Ganeswar, *op. cit.*, p. 67.
90. *AGROD, 1882-83*, p. 56.
91. Nayak, Ganeswar, *op. cit.*, pp. 67-69.
92. Samal, J.K., *op. cit.*, p. 167.
93. Maddox, S.L., *op. cit.*, p. 23.
94. *BODG: Cuttack*, p. 108.
95. *AGAROD, 1894-95*, p. 49.
96. *Ibid.*
97. *RABO, 1912-1913*, p. 71.
98. *Ibid., 1915-1916*, p. 69.
99. *BODG: Cuttack*, p. 105
100. *Report on the Administration of Bengal, 1890-91*, *op. cit.*, p. 24.
101. *RABO, 1915-1916*, p. 67.
102. *Ibid., 1917-18*, p. 73.
103. *Ibid., 1919-1920*, p. 62.
104. *Ibid., 1920-1921*, p. 26.
105. *Ibid.*, p. 27.

106. *Bihar and Orissa First Decennial Review, 1912-1922*, Government of Bihar and Orissa, Patna, 1923, p. 2.
107. *Ibid.*
108. *Bihar and Orissa in 1927-28*, Government of Bihar and Orissa, Patna, 1929, p. 83.
109. *Bihar and Orissa in 1929-30,* Government of Bihar and Orissa, Patna, 1931, p. 93.
110. *BODG: Cuttack*, p. 105.
111. Mahapatra, Jadu Nath, *op. cit.*, p. 131.
112. Nayak, Ganeswar, *op. cit.*, p. 69.
113. *BODG: Cuttack*, p. 105.
114. *AGAROD, 1885-86,* p. 44.
115. *Ibid., 1886-87*, p. 42.
116. *Ibid.,1887-88*, p. 35.
117. *SCRO,* 1945-46, pp. 6-7.
118. *Report on the Administration of Bengal, 1890-91*, *op. cit.*, p. 24.
119. *Report of the Land Revenue Administration of the Lower Provinces for the year 1906-1907*, The Bengal Secretariat Book Depot, Calcutta, 1907, p. 18.
120. *Report on the Land Revenue Administration of the Lower Provinces for the year 1907-1908*, Government of Bengal, Calcutta, 1908, p. 17.
121. *Ibid.*
122. *Report on the Land Revenue Administration of the Lower Provinces for the year 1908-1909*, Government of Bengal, Calcutta, 1909, p. 14.
123. *Report on the Administration of Bihar and Orissa, 1912-1913*, Government of Bihar and Orissa, Patna, 1914, p. 71.
124. *RABO, 1915-1916*, pp. 67.
125. *Ibid., 1917-1918*, p. 73.
126. *Ibid., 1918-1919*, p. 74.
127. *Ibid.*
128. *Ibid., 1919-1920*, p. 63.
129. *Ibid.* p. 62.
130. *Bihar and Orissa First Decennial Review, 1912-1922*, Government of Bihar and Orissa, Patna, 1923, p. 2.
131. *BODG: Cuttack*, p. 105.
132. Mahapatra, Jadu Nath, *op. cit.*, p. 131.

3

Impact of the Canal Irrigation on the Agrarian Economy of Coastal Orissa

> Misunderstanding of the present grows fatally from the ignorance of the past. —*Marc Bloch*[1]

EXPANSION OF CANAL IRRIGATION

The colonialist started canal irrigation keeping all their desired fundamental objectives in internal thoughts. With the course of time canal irrigation expanded in coastal Orissa. It continued in a full swing till 1918-19. By 1900-01, it crossed 2 lakhs of acres and by 1918-19 it touched nearer 3 lakhs of acres of land. After 1918-19 expansion became slow and its percentage came down owing to floods, low profits, and several other factors. In order to understand the expansion of canal irrigation bar diagrams have been used along with the division of the long span of period from 1878-79 to 1946-47 into few time groups. In order to understand the real situation peasants voices are primarily highlighted from different colonial records.

Interestingly with the expansion of canal, the cultivation of commercialised crops went up side by side till the independence which itself suggests that there was a new trend of agriculture, that can be regarded as the age of commercialisation of agriculture in coastal Orissa. Canal actually compelled the peasants to go for that kind of cultivation through the key of water tax and outer market demands. Peasants were promised to get high production by using canal water, but the expectation of high production could not come true to them. Till independence no improvement of the standard of the peasants was seen. Above all, their claim of the improvement of agriculture and the stoppage of the failure of crop were all vague for the poor peasants of colonial coastal Orissa.

The Orissa canal system actually started irrigating agricultural land from 1869-70. However, it was confined to Cuttack district then. Thus, the period 1860-61 had 1,729 acres of land irrigated. In the 1870-71 period saw a huge leap in the acres of land irrigated, it was 22,128 acres; mainly, the low rainfall contributed to it.[2] In 1871-72, the total lands that come under canal cultivation was 11,653 acres which was less than the previous year and it further reduced 4,753 acres[3] in the next year. As per the Administrative records of 1873-74 around 4,853 acres of land brought under the canal irrigation by 1872-73, but it rose to 12,571 acres by 1873-74.[4] Again in the next year (1874-75), it was almost doubled to 22,796 acres.[5] However, it came down in 1875-76 period to 17,999 acres (18,409 acres as per 1875-76 administration record).[6] But suddenly the amount of irrigated area went up to 30,233 acres in the next year (1876-77).[7] This was increased almost thrice to 98,495 acres during the period 1877-78. For the first time the canal irrigation system introduced in Balasore district from the third range of the High level canal. Till then, the canal irrigation system was confined to the Cuttack district only, whereas there was no irrigation work in Puri district.[8] In the year 1877-78, the area brought under the canal irrigation system was 98,495 acres.[9] But the report of 1878-79 tells the actual amount was 97,261 acres as 1,234 acres of land was under unauthorized irrigation (those who did not lease for canal irrigation).[10] Comparing to preceding years the amount was high just because the rainfall was scanty and peasants were compelled to depend on canal water for irrigation.[11]

Table 3.1 gives the statistics of the total number of acres of agricultural land irrigated through the canal irrigation system from 1869-70 to 1877-78:

Table 3.1: Total Canal Irrigated Land

(in acres)

Year	*Land*
1869-70	1,729
1870-71	22,128
1871-72	11,653
1872-73	4,753
1873-74	12,571
1874-75	22,459
1875-76	18,409
1876-77	30,382
1877-78	98,495

Source: General Administration Report of Orissa Division from 1873-74 to 1876-77; Annual General Administration Report, Orissa Division from 1877-78 to 1878-79.

Below given a bar diagram presentation of the same to understand the fluctuations clearly.

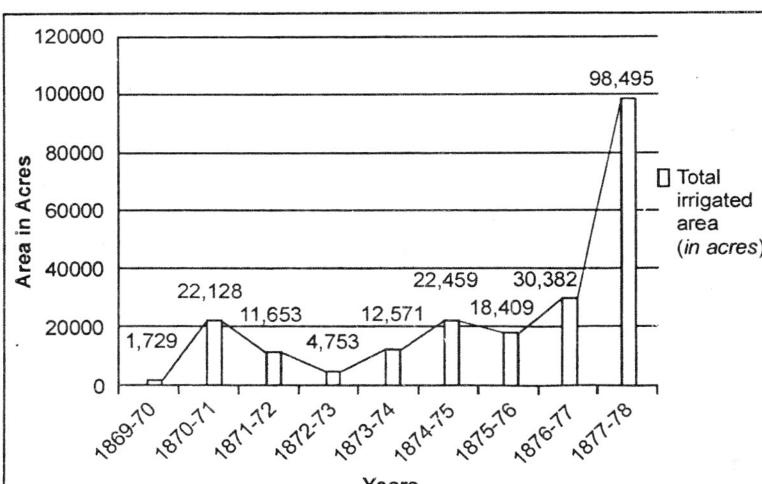

Fig. 3.1: Total Canal Irrigated area from 1869-70 to 1877-78 (in acres).

Table 3.1 indicates fluctuations in the use of canal irrigation. From the year one to two there was a sharp leap, and then the next period it witnesses a fall in the use almost by half. The period 1872-73, there was a sharp decline and it reaches the 1871-72 position in the year 1873-74. The canal water usage was corresponding with the amount of rainfall received. Whenever, there was a good monsoon, the canal water usage for irrigation has been reduced considerably. This is natural. For example in 1871-72, Cuttack has received 50.03 inches rains, whereas in Balasore 84.69 inches and Puri 49.79 inches. In 1872-73 when the canal water usage was the lowest ever, Cuttack recorded 72.53 inches rains, Balasore 71.10 inches, Puri 72.61 inches.[12] Low rainfall in 1873-74 was real cause for the little increase in the canal irrigated land.[13] The process of declination repeated back again in 1875-76 due to favourable rainfall which caused in the decrease of leased lands.[14] Between 1876-77 and 1877-78, there was a huge leap. Total proportion of irrigated land went up all of a sudden. This could be attributed to the monsoon failure in Cuttack, Poree and partially in Balasore.[15]

But by the next year, the amount of irrigated land went up to 1,00,263 acres.[16] Since in Balasore canal irrigation was newly introduced, by 1882-83 the irrigated land amount was only 1,585 acres.[17] But in case of Cuttack district, the case was different; it recorded only a marginal increase in terms of acres of land. The total amount of canal irrigated land was 1,32,067 acres (for 1882-83) against the last year's amount1,30,408 acres.[18] The amount of land declined drastically to 48,359 acres next year, out of which 45,981 acres belonged to Cuttack district and the rest belonged to Balasore district. This drastic downfall was attributed to the expiry of five year leases in November 1882.[19] But as per the report of 1884-85, the amount of canal irrigated land was in the Balasore district 2,585 acres.[20] Next year the number increased to 2,971 acres. In Cuttack, the number of acres was 54,401 for the same period. So both together the total number of acres for the year 1884-85 was 57,372.[21] However, by the end of 1886, the total irrigated area increased to 72,339 acres. Out of which 65,533 acres were from Cuttack district and the remaining 6,806 acres was from Balasore district.[22] During the year 1886-87, the proportion of irrigated area increased to 78,035 acres, of which 6,211 acres only belonged to Balasore district.[23] In 1887-88, 1,09,506 acres of land brought under the canal irrigation against 77,709 acres of land last year.[24] This increase was due to the low rainfall. As for the district of Puri, canal irrigation was not begun till then. Traditional irrigational methods continued there and the government spent money from the Miscellaneous Improvement Fund, the Khas Mahal Fund, and Agricultural Improvement Fund[25] for the improvisation of the traditional methods of irrigation. Table 3.2 and Fig. 3.2 shows the total canal irrigated area for the ten years ending 1887-88.

Table 3.2: Total Canal Irrigated Area from 1878-79 to 1887-88

Year	*Total canal irrigated area (in acres)*
1878-79	1,00,263
1879-80	NA
1880-81	NA
1881-82	1,30,408
1882-83	1,32,067
1883-84	48,368
1884-85	57,372
1885-86	72,339
1886-87	78,035
1887-88	1,09,506

Note: NA = Data is not available.

Source: Annual General Report for Orissa Division from 1878-79 to 1887-88.

Table 3.2 shows a sharp increase in the irrigated land's proportion till 1882-83. It was so because of the water rate to Rs. 3 for the land which was under the short period of lease.[26] In addition to this, there was around 1,585 acres of land which was leased[27] and a five years lease was in force which lasted only in 1882.[28] But, all of a

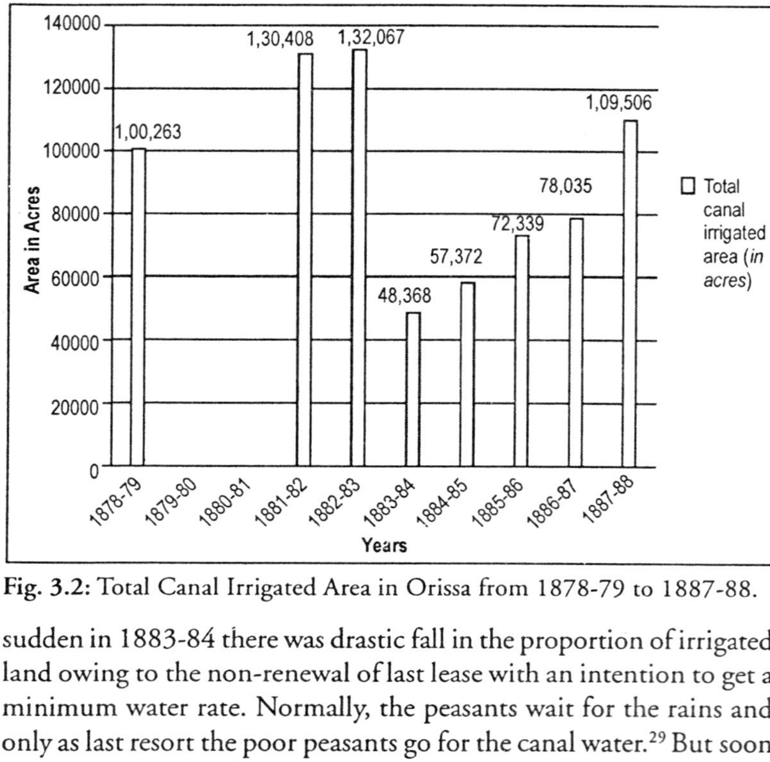

Fig. 3.2: Total Canal Irrigated Area in Orissa from 1878-79 to 1887-88.

sudden in 1883-84 there was drastic fall in the proportion of irrigated land owing to the non-renewal of last lease with an intention to get a minimum water rate. Normally, the peasants wait for the rains and only as last resort the poor peasants go for the canal water.[29] But soon it started resuming the process of sharp increase which continued to till the end of 1887-88. It was not that the poor peasants were all happy to take water from canal system but because of the gradual rise of the amount of leased area apprehending the failure of crops (example failure of crop in Khorda subdivision in 1887). Side by side there was expansion of canal system. Out of the last all nineteen years only in1882-83 had the highest share ever in this regard.

For the year 1888-89, the amount of the total irrigated area increased to 1,56,312 acres.[30] As per the administration report of 1890-91, the total area came under the canal irrigation was 1,75,412 acres during 1889-90.[31] The next year the amount of land increased to 1,94,318 acres (for 1890-91).[32] During 1892-93, the total irrigated area was 1,60,952 acres. The drought of 1888 compelled the Orissa peasants to go under an agreement which lasted till 1892-93. For few succeeding years rainfall was copious due to this the total irrigated area from the canal came down to 1,03,526 acres during 1893-94, and this amount of land slightly went up to 1,22,561 acres during 1894-95.[33] It was almost stabilized and by 1895-96, the amount of land was 1,20,821 acres. There was sharp increase recorded in the amount of land irrigated by canal in the period 1896-97 to 1,86,048 acres and in 1897-98 it further increased to 1,93,600 acres.[34] And again the amount of land under canal irrigation reached to 2,03,033 acres during 1899-1900.[35] Table 3.3 shows the total canal irrigated areas for the above twelve years from 1888-89 to 1899-1900:

Table 3.3: Total Irrigated area

(in acres)

Year	*Irrigated Land*
1888-89	1,56,312
1889-90	1,75,412
1890-91	1,94,318
1891-92	NA
1892-93	1,60,952
1893-94	1,03,526
1894-95	1,22,561
1895-96	1,20,821
1896-97	1,86,048
1897-98	1,93,600
1898-99	NA
1899-1900	2,03,033

Note: NA = Data not available.

Source: Annual General Administration Report of Orissa Division from 1888-89 to 1899-1900.

From the bar diagram (Fig. 3.3), it is clear that there were too many fluctuations during these twelve years. The previous pace of increase remained intact till 1890-91. It was so because of the

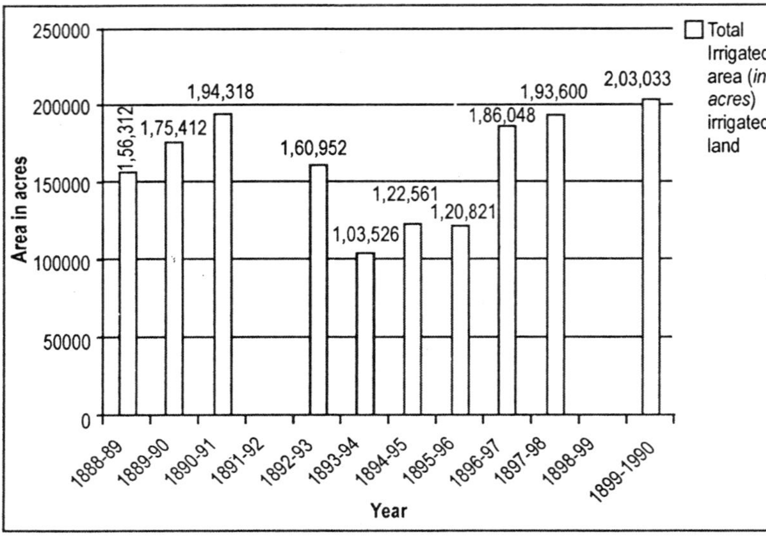

Fig. 3.3: Total Canal Irrigated Area from 1888-89 to 1899-1900 (in acres).

insufficient rainfall in the preceding years.[36] From 1891-92, the process of declination resumed on its way. It was just because there was good rainfall. But this did not last for long. From the period 1893-94, it began to increase. And the variation is negligible since then for the next three years. 1899-1900 period saw it touching the highest point. It was attributed to the execution of new leases and also to the poor rainfall. From 1895-96 rainfall in slight low pace[37] which had created a phobia of the loss of crop among the peasants. Unfortunately data is not available for the period from 1900 to till 1912-13.

In the year 1911-12, around 2,79,225 acres of land was under the canal irrigation system and during 1912-13, this was declined slightly to 2,76,414 acres of land.[38] Again there was a marginal increase to 2,82,564 acres during 1914-15 and in 1915-16, it almost maintained the 1912-13; 27,626 acres of land was irrigated by canal system.[39] In short, during the period 1912 to 1918, slight variations were witnessed in the amount of land irrigated under the canal system

(1916-17, 2,78,065 acres and 1917-18 it was 2,71,576 acres).[40] Owing to the unfavourable rainfall little more area of land was brought under the canal cultivation whose amount reached to 2,85,199 acres during 1918-19.[41] The total amount of land which was under the canal irrigation system during 1919-20 was 2,89,835 acres.[42] So in the nine years starting from 1911-12 to 1919-20, the total canal irrigated lands statistics would be:

Table 3.4: Total Canal Irrigated Land

(*in acres*)

Year	*Irrigated land*
1910-11	NA
1911-12	2,79,225
1912-13	2,76,414
1913-14	NA
1914-15	2,82,564
1915-16	2,76,264
1916-17	2,78,065
1917-18	2,71,576
1918-19	2,85,199
1919-20	2,89,835

Note: NA = Data is not available.

Source: Report on the Administration of Bihar and Orissa from 1911-12 to 1919-20.

As per the above statistics the diagram is shown in Fig. 3.4 .

Unlike the period between 1878-88 and 1888-1900, the variation in the amount of land irrigated from the canal during the period from 1910-11 to 1919-20 was marginal. The previous period witnessed huge fluctuations.

In 1920-21, there was a marginal increase in the total land which was irrigated by canal system from the previous year to 2,92,084 acres.[43] Data was not available for the period between 1921-22 and 1926-27. In 1927-28, the total land which was irrigated by Orissa canal system was 2,50,384 acres.[44] For the year 1929-30 saw a decrease

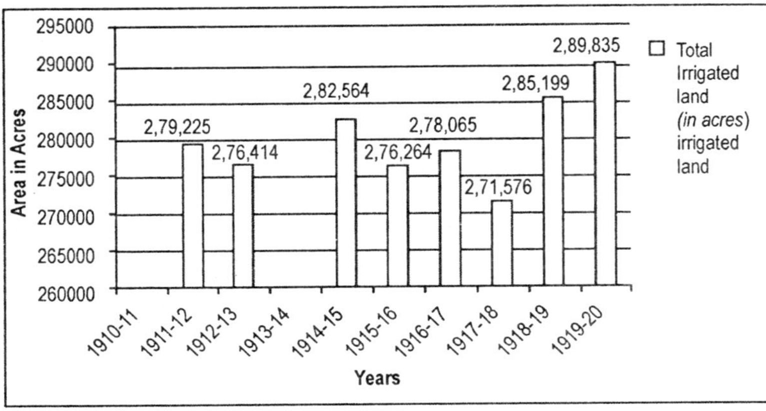

Fig. 3.4: Total Canal Irrigated Land from 1911-12 to 1919-20 (in acres).

in the number of acres of canal irrigated land.[45] But in the very next financial year (1930-31), there was keen demand for water, particularly in the month of July and August.[46]

As no segregated data is available in this regard in the context of Orissa from 1931-32 to 1935-36, it is necessary go through the records of united data of Bihar and Orissa province. In 1931-32, the total area irrigated by canal water was 8,77,658 acres in the province of Bihar and Orissa.[47] But by the next year, the amount of land was little higher than that of 1931-32. It was around 8,93,000 acres in 1932-33.[48] During 1933-34, the number had declined to 8,69,250 acres.[49] Including both *kharif* and *rabi* seasons, the land that was irrigated by canal system both in the province of Bihar and Orissa was 8,52,727 acres.[50]

On April 1, 1936, Orissa became separate province.[51] From then onwards, Orissa had separate records from administration point of view. Hence, it became easier to access all records separately in the context of Orissa. The total area irrigated by canal system in 1936-37 was 2,02,552 acres. In the next year (1937-38), it came down to 1,94,702 acres and there was a slight increase in the year preceded; it reached to 2,04,483 acres.[52] The total irrigated area increased again in 1939-40 to 2,38,978 acres.[53] In the year 1941-42 witnessed a marginal decrease and the number went down to 2,38,370 acres.[54] Data was not available for the period 1942-43 and it is not difficult to assume from the trend that there would not a drastic change in the figure for the period. In 1943-44, the total irrigated area under canal system was 2,61,370 acres.[55] And there was an increase to 2,63,970 acres of irrigated land in 1944-45.[56] Since then, the figure remains stagnated till the period 1946-47 and the country got independence in the same year.[57]

It will be interesting to look at those above eleven years from 1936-37 to 1946-47 total canal irrigated land under the British India government:

Table 3.5: Total Canal Irrigated Land

(in acres)

Year	*Irrigated Land*
1936-37	2,02,552
1937-38	1,94,702
1938-39	2,04,483
1939-40	2,38,978
1940-41	NA
1941-42	2,38,370
1942-43	NA
1943-44	2,61,370
1944-45	2,63,970
1945-46	2,63,970
1946-47	2,63,970

Note: NA = Data not available

Source: Orissa from 1936-37 to 1938-39; Season and Crop Report from 1939-40 to 1944-45; Report on the Land Revenue Administration of the districts of North Orissa for the year 1946-47.

According to the above statistics the bar diagram is shown as Fig. 3.5.

From the above shown 11 years' data, it is very clear that after 1919-20, the total irrigated land had been decreased. The decline

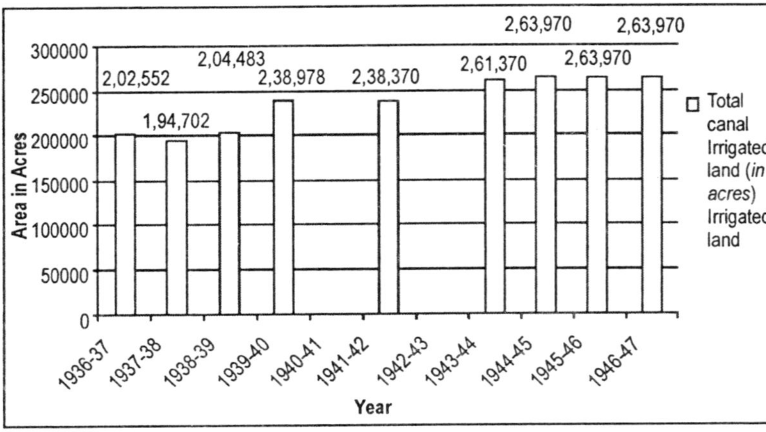

Fig. 3.5: Total Canal Irrigated Land (in acres) from 1936-37 to 1946-47.

was attributed to reasonably good rainfall. From 1937-38 its proportion sharply increased till 1939-40 taking rainfall as its back force. In 1936-37, recorded rainfall was 76.39 inches; however, from the next year onwards it started to decline from 57.30 inches in 1937-38 to 55.61 inches in 1938-39.[58] But in 1941-42, it had received better rainfall and this was reflected in the number of acres irrigated by the canal system.[59] In 1944-45, the total irrigated land maintained little highest out of few preceding years. But the area under the canal irrigation remained same till 1946-47, without any alteration. This could be attributed to the consistent monsoon.

Overall, the whole above narration has clearly proved that only at the time of low rainfall peasants went for canal irrigation and in the normal years peasants did not go for this kind of irrigation. This very statement makes the sense that peasants' disliking was there too much during the colonial period not because they were conservative as was revealed from the colonialist record or had apathetic attitude towards agricultural development but by felling at canal's real nature.

THE MYTH OF THE DEVELOPMENT OF AGRICULTURE

There was an argument built up, especially by the colonialist that the introduction of the canal irrigation in India helped to step up the agricultural development took place along with increased production, and the Indian peasants benefited out of it enormously.[60] They claimed that overall it opened a new path to maximize their income. And also canal irrigation helped to reclaim vast stretched wasteland. But on the contrary, the reality was something else. While this proposition was made by the imperialist school, the peasant participation was not taken into account. With that the gradual growth of population and their gradual demand on agriculture was completely deleted from their account, which ultimately shows that they wanted to create a positive picture of them in front of the common man.[61] The canal irrigation was their main attributing factor for different kinds of development.[62]

Pertaining to Orissa, where an extensive canal system had been built, similar arguments were presented by the imperialist historians. On the contrary, the peasant voiced that these claims were shallow and there was no marked improvement in the agricultural sector. Interestingly, the *Final Report on the Survey and Settlement of the Province of Orissa, 1890 to 1900* by S.L. Maddox reflected the mood of the people. It assertively said:

> In the opinion of many and certainly in that of the Oriya peasants the chief value of canal water lies not in any improvement but in the protection which it affords against total or partial failure in the years of drought.[63]

The same record exposed the high claim that the canal system step up the expansion of agricultural land and thus the production. The report clearly stated that there was not any kind of substantial extension of cultivation because of canal irrigation. It further stated:

> It will be seen that the increase of cultivation is certainly no greater in the protected and irrigated groups, and all the enquiries made have failed to elicit any evidence of a substantial extension of cultivation to lands which but for the canal water were not likely to have been reclaimed. It is of course certain that some lands, such as the sand-damaged areas in *Kodinda* have been reclaimed, which, without canal water, would not pay for cultivation.[64]

It was just because the people out of their needs extended their agricultural land by clearing wasteland, but not because of the canal irrigation.[65] There are other records, by the British officials that refuted the big claims of colonial bureaucrats that the canal irrigation helped to expand the agriculture land. For instance L.S.S. O'Malley stated in the *Bihar and Orissa District Gazetteers* that:

> The canal system does not appear to have been a special cause in the extension of cultivation; the increase has been no greater in the protected and irrigated areas than elsewhere; and the enquiries made on the subject have failed to elicit any evidence of a substantial extension of cultivation to lands which but for the canal water were not likely to have been reclaimed.[66]

It reiterated the statement of S.L. Maddox, on the subject matter.[67] Even in 1939-40, it was recorded by Jadu Nath Mahapatra that, the Oriya peasants used to consider the newly devised irrigation method as an insurance against drought, not as a regular method of irrigation or a source of agricultural development.[68] It is evident from the records that it was the monsoon failure that forced the peasants to draw water from the canals for irrigation for a price. Whenever, the rainfall blessed them then forgot about the existence of the canal which is clearly seen from the decline of canal irrigated land.

IMPACT ON CROPPING PATTERN: THE AGE OF COMMERCIALISATION OF AGRICULTURE

In history, sometimes, impact of an event or a set of events felt after a very long duration. So in order to understand a particular event it is necessary in that case to observe the particular event or set of events over a long period of time (Annals historiography's concept of long duration, quantitative observation of historical trends is more or less essential to the history of the *longue duree*).[69] Out of those kinds of events, the reference here is about agriculture; the fact that the impact of the commercialisation of agriculture felt after a long time. This section will discuss about such impacts as commercialisation of agriculture, however, unfortunately, very few records are available in this regard to understand the complete course of history of commercialisation of agriculture and its impacts on agriculture in coastal Orissa. Before going into such a discussion, it is pertinent here to understand the major difference between the commercial crops and subsistence crops. The major difference being that the commercial crops are cultivated for the need of market whereas the subsistence crops are cultivated for consumption purpose. Examples of commercial crops are tobacco, cotton, jute, sugar and indigo etc. But subsistence crops include mostly the food crops. More importantly, the subsistence crops ensured food security.

There were a number of reasons for the commercialisation of agriculture in Orissa. One of the major reasons was that the demand for payment of high land revenue in cash put huge pressure on the peasantry to produce cash crops for the market, in addition to the subsistence crops for the household consumption.[70] For example jute cultivation in eastern India developed as the peasants failed to meet the subsistence necessities and hoped to earn more by cultivating the "golden crop" (jute).[71] Compared to food crops, the commercial crops fetched higher prices. Hence, Orissa peasants looked at the cultivation of commercial as a way to face the oppressive land tax.[72] In addition to that, they were also burdened with irrigational charges. The occasional famine like the one that hit in 1866 played havoc in their lives. During the famine of 1866 and the post famine period, many peasants were evicted from their land. Some of the small and middle peasants sold their land or mortgaged it to the *Zamindars* which made them *pahir yots (pahir yots* were non-resident cultivators and *thanir yots* were resident cultivators).[73] This kind of apprehension created a mental phobia among the Orissa peasants. This is the context the canal irrigation system entered and the peasants gradually turned to commercial crops to meet their immediate needs of paying land along with water tax in cash. In fact, the peasants aligned to the priorities and aspirations of western masters. The spread of commercial crops which projected to bring revenue stability was one among them.[74]

Attempts of the Colonial Government for Popularising Commercial Crops

The British government devised certain strategies for the spread of commercial crops all-over Orissa. One among them was setting up agricultural research centres, particularly on different kinds of commercial crops, in different geographical zones.[75] Agricultural farms were also established with the same motive.[76] For example, within Orissa 65 varieties of sugarcane and also several varieties of paddy were cultivated.[77] As per Jadu Nath Mahapatra, to popularise commercial crops among the Oriya peasants, the British even adopted the policy of reduction of water rate. The best example to illustrate this is the water tax cut in Cuttack district from the rate Rs. 2 per acre to Rs. 1/2 per acre, in order to expand the cultivation of jute in irrigated areas. And it was also highly hoped by the colonialists that Oriya peasants would appreciate the concession and increase the cultivation of the jute crop.[78] But unfortunately, the Oriya people did not understand their evil intention in this regard.

In fact, in Orissa, the British introduced commercial crop for their benefit by 1830s itself. However, the early attempts to introduce commercial crops, particularly indigo and cotton did not met with success as expected. This was so owing to the unsuitable environment for such crops.[79] Still to some extent, it was succeeded. One of the early statistics for the commercial crops came from the records of Cuttack district. Table 3.6 shows the increase of commercial crops in the district of Cuttack during the mid-eighteenth century:

Table 3.6: Total Area under Commercial Crops

(in acres)

Crop	*Before settlement of 1837*	*In 1858*
Sugarcane	312	709
Cotton	3,020	6,474
Tobacco	1,723	2,744
Total	**5,055**	**9,927**

Source: Pradipta Chaudhury, "Peasants and British Rule in Orissa", *Social Scientist*, Vol. 19, No. 8/9, Aug.-Sep., 1991, pp. 40-41.

Table 3.6 shows that from 1837 to 1858, except for tobacco, the area of cultivation of sugarcane and cotton was more than doubled. There was considerable expansion in tobacco production too. As per the same record, the total area under the cotton crop cultivated by 1894-95 was 6,100 acres; this was indeed a marginal decline. Next year it further declined to 5,900 acres and it further reduced to 5,300 acre during 1896-97 periods.[80] During 1896-97, the total share of commercial crops out of total exports was close to 3 per cent. During 1898-99, it was about 5 per cent of the total export. The share increased to nearly 8 per cent by the mid of 1900.[81] That statistics itself suggests that the demand for commercial crop increased year by year steadily. In that export list some of the commercial crops were mentioned such as jute, cotton, tobacco, indigo, silk, sugar, linseed, tea and mustard seed. Though the share of food crops (subsistence crop) was high, still the importance of the presence of commercial crops cannot be ignored. From this it is clear that Orissa peasants used to cultivate commercial crops side by side of the subsistence crops.

By 1900, peasants in the three coastal districts of Orissa were familiar with different kinds of commercial crops though its share was small.[82] With the tide of time it reached to a very high point. In Balasore district, as per the agricultural statistics, the total percentage of commercial crops along with other non-food items was nearer to 10 per cent out of the total cultivation.[83] It itself stands as a symbol for the rise of the cultivation of commercialised crops. The Cuttack district was not an exception. Cuttack district witnessed a significant rise in jute production.[84] Out of all kinds of commercialised crops jute percentage was high. It was cultivated in 4,300 acres in the Balasore district.[85] In Puri district, out of total cultivated area, while around 7,36,800 acres of land was dedicated for subsistence crop out of the total cultivated area of 8,25,700 acres; the commercial crops claimed the rest amount of cultivable land. Sugarcane was cultivated over 2,500 acres of land, tobacco around over 400 acres of land, cotton over 500 acres of land and so on.[86] Sugarcane was grown in the whole district here and there. Along with Bihar, Orissa maintained the status of third largest sugarcane growing province in India and both the provinces used to produce nearly half of white sugar produced in the country.[87] Tobacco was an important crop in some parts, particularly Dandimal region, Narasinghapur region and Cuttack – Puri road area. Its production was such that people used to trade tobacco, to Calcutta. Similarly indigo was also used to be grown in this district but in small quantities in the headquarters subdivision.[88] There are many records available that claim that the direct intervention of the British improved the agriculture in Orissa. The introduction of different new crops was one of their claims it was one of the exclusive assignments of the agricultural department.[89]

Table 3.7 gives information on a number of crops—sugar, cotton, tobacco, jute, oil seeds, fruit and vegetables—for the period 1912-13 to 1943-44.

Table 3.7 indicates that the cultivation of different kinds of commercial crops was in full swing till 1932-33 and after it continued last few years in a declining trend.

By 1931-32, the area under oil seeds including mustard had

Table 3.7: Total Area under Commercial Crops Still 1942-43

(in acres)

			Tobacco				
Districts	*1912-13*	*1917-18*	*1922-23*	*1927-28*	*1932-33*	*1937-38*	*1942-43*
Cuttack	6,600	6,100	6,800	9,300	9,700	5,682	4,690
Balasore	100	200	200	200	100	60	100
Puri	200	400	400	200	200	110	75
			Jute				
Districts	*1912-13*	*1917-18*	*1922-23*	*1927-28*	*1932-33*	*1937-38*	*1942-43*
Cuttack	12,000	20,700	16,200	15,800	17,200	14,200	21,400
Balasore	3,400	2,100	1,500	2,800	2,000	1,100	1,800
Puri	NA	NA	NA	NA	NA	310	600
			Fruits and Vegetables				
Districts	*1912-13*	*1917-18*	*1922-23*	*1927-28*	*1932-33*	*1937-38*	*1942-43*
Cuttack	84,000	84,000	81,500	94,000	89,800	40,504	18,500
Balasore	50,000	50,000	50,000	50,000	15,200	9,340	11,000
Puri	75,300	75,600	50,100	50,100	50,100	75,630	75,630
			Cotton				
Districts	*1912-13*	*1917-18*	*1922-23*	*1927-28*	*1932-33*	*1937-38*	*1942-43*
Cuttack	2,600	2,000	2,900	1,000	1,100	5,005	5,130
Balasore	300	20	100	100	15		
Puri	400	400	500	500	400	80	212
			Sugarcane				
Districts	*1912-13*	*1917-18*	*1922-23*	*1927-28*	*1932-33*	*1937-38*	*1942-43*
Cuttack	3,000	3,200	2,800	3,300	3,100	6,555	7,500
Balasore	2,100	1,600	1,800	1,400	1,400	1,350	1,600
Puri	2,300	2,400	2,400	2,400	3,000	3,881	3,441
			Oilseeds				
Districts	*1912-13*	*1917-18*	*1922-23*	*1927-28*	*1932-33*	*1937-38*	*1942-43*
Cuttack	30,200	14,100	17,300	19,500	17,500	34,555	36,850
Balasore	11,200	4,600	7,900	9,000	4,500	2,275	2,310
Puri	6,400	8,300	35,400	35,000	35,000	32,187	32,537

Source: Rajib Lochan Sahoo (2004). *Agrarian Change and Peasant Unrest in Colonial India, Orissa 1912-1939*, Manak Publication, New Delhi, pp. 163-70.[90]

increased from 47 to 95 acres in every 10,000 acres of land. Cotton growing had dwindled into complete insignificance. Other valuable crops like jute, sugarcane, and *pan* had advanced in a very marked manner. The area under betel leaf had increased from 469 acres in 1900 to 1,108 acres since the provincial settlement by S.L. Maddox. This increase happened because one new place was brought under the settlement of 1922-32, namely Kujang by Dalziel. Tobacco cultivation had decreased. Jute was grown on two acres in every thousand acres of land (known from W.W. Dalziel's Final Report on the Revision Settlement of Orissa 1922-32).[91]

The area under cultivation of tobacco and gram steadily increased till 1938-39, as it was mentioned by Jadu Nath Mahapatra. Coming to sugarcane, in 1936-37, the total land devoted to this crop was 31,385 acres. By next year, it had increased to 34,834 acres. But it declined to 32,020 acres in 1938-39. Similarly in the case of jute, Cuttack and Balasore were the hubs. The area that was devoted to this crop was 13,500 acres in 1936-37; however, this was reduced to 15,610 acres in 1937-38 and further declined by the next year.[92] The data shows that even till 1938-39, the cultivation of commercial crops still had remained in an important position as far as agrarian history of Orissa was concerned. In 1939-40, the total commercial crop area was 2,18,870 acres out of total cultivated area of 31,25,406 acres in the three coastal districts of Orissa.[93] Though overall its share was only 7 per cent, but the area of commercial crops increased considerably. Puri district had the highest share of commercial crops around 12 per cent whereas Cuttack district comes next with nearly 8 per cent. Though Cuttack district had highest amount of land under the commercial crop but comparing to its total cultivation its share was less. Balasore district had only a small area under commercial crop, which was less than 2 per cent.

During 1941-42 the total commercial crop cultivated area was 1,70,211 acres out of 31,55,392 acres, a share of 5.39 per cent of the total cultivated area. In Cuttack district, 76,800 acres of land was totally devoted for commercial crops, this was more than 5 per cent of the total cultivated area of that year. Similarly in Balasore district,

6,600 acres of land was under different kinds of commercial crops, which was around 0.73 per cent of the total cultivated area. Puri district was not an exception to this matter. It had highest share of 11.19 per cent commercial crop of the total cultivated area. The amount of the commercial crop area was 86,811 acres[94], which was little higher in 1939-40. In 1943-44, land available for the commercial crop decreased to 1,20,070 acres (3.70%) out of the total cropped area of 32,38,228 acres of land. Even district-wise its share decreased. In Cuttack, 76,810 acres of land out of 15,11,683 acres of land, around 5.08 per cent; in Balasore district, 6,260 acres of land out of 9,13,463 acres of land for the entire cultivation, this constituted around 0.68 per cent; and in Puri district, 37,000 acres of land out of 8,13,082 acres of land, around 4.55 per cent was devoted for different commercial crops.[95] In 1944-45, the total amount of commercial crop area decreased to 99,273 acres (3%), out of the total cultivated area of 33,15,083 acres. In Cuttack district, 81,900 acres of land was under the commercial crops out of 15,91,000 acres of land. Similarly, 7,965 acres of land out of 9,23,735 acres of total cultivated area was under commercial crops in Balasore, and 19,408 acres of land out of 8,00,348 acres of total cultivated area was under commercial crops. The share of Balasore in relation to the total cropped area was below 1 per cent whereas in case of Puri it was 2.5 per cent.[96] During the year 1945-46, the total commercial crop cultivated land was 1,05,765 acres, which was around below 4 per cent of the total cultivated area, 33,38,029 acres. In that year, Cuttack stood at the forefront of commercial crop cultivation. The district had total cultivation of 78,520 acres of commercial crops. It was little above 5 per cent of the total cultivated area of that year in that district. Similarly in Balasore district 7,385 acres (below 2% of the total cultivated land) and Puri district 19,860 acres (below 3% of the total cultivated land).[97]

From Table 3.8, it is clear that though overall there was a decreasing tendency of the cultivation of commercial crops still that cultivation remained intact. This proportion came down steadily, it was because the total cultivated area increased (because of reclamation

Table 3.8: Total Average Share of Commercial Crops Cultivation

(*in percentage*)

Years	*Dist. Average share out of total cultivation*			*Total share of commercial crops*
	Cuttack	*Balasore*	*Puri*	
1939-40	7.85	1.69	11.91	7.00
1941-42	5.17	0.73	11.19	5.39
1943-44	5.08	0.68	4.55	3.70
1944-45	5.14	0.86	2.42	2.99
1945-46	5.02	1.84	2.38	3.16

Note: The data for the years 1940-41 and 1942-43 is not available.
Source: *Season and crop Reports of Orissa from 1939-40 to 1945-46.*

of wasteland lands) and the cultivation of commercialised crops did not go up much. Puri district indicates a drastic downfall in the cultivation of commercial crops. Mostly it was for the fact that the Puri district did not have canal irrigation facility and hence the colonialists did not pressurise the farmers of that district to cultivate commercial crops. But Cuttack district remained intact more or less in this regard. And in the context of Balasore district its proportion increased. It was so because of the very good communication system it had both in navigable canal and railways.

Now, the whole above narrative makes the sense here is that, there was the beginning of a new age of commercialisation of agriculture as far as agrarian history of coastal Orissa is concerned. Before the introduction of canal irrigation these commercial crops did not dominate the region's agriculture and with the canal irrigation, it started going up and continued till even the last hour of independence. This took a special position in the agrarian section of Orissa. This special cultivation profited much to the British as they made this region a procurement area of agricultural raw materials for their market and for industrial need also. Again the colonial rulers' high need of those commercial crops has been proved by the new rapid trend of transportation of commercial crops, on which a separate discussion has been placed in the next chapter.

IMPACT OF CANAL IRRIGATION ON AGRICULTURAL PRODUCTION

Coming to the impact of canal irrigation on the agrarian production, the imperialist historians maintained a strong and bold claim that agricultural production increased due to the canal irrigation in India. According to Morris D. Morris and W.H. Moreland, due to different British economic policies per capita agricultural production increased.[98] This increase was attributed to the introduction of canal irrigation in the master's records. In Colonel Haig's note of 1877, it was noted that the value of the paddy in irrigated land increased which was equal with 15.69 maunds (a unit of weight averagely of 37 kg.) of paddy.[99] An estimate by the Canal Irrigation Committee of 1884 showed that the production in the canal irrigated land increased in comparison with non-irrigated land. As per his estimates, there was a difference of 5 maunds per acre in between dry land and wetland.[100] Similarly, in another decennial period (1885-86 to 1896-97), experiment showed that the average production of paddy from irrigated land was 19.7 maunds whereas in case of non-irrigated land, it was only 15.59 maunds of paddy.[101] In Puri district, the average production per acre was 14 maunds in general, 17 maunds per acre in Pipli area in particular.[102] Even in 1930-31, once again the British claimed that the average production of paddy during that period was 19 maunds per acre.[103] Similarly another record revealed that the outcome of clean rice per acre was 13½ maunds for irrigated lands and 12 maunds for non-irrigated lands.[104]

So, what actually happened in the whole argument here is that there was no unanimity among the opinions of the colonialists, which itself partially proves that they wanted to hide something from the eyes of the poor peasants or must had the colonialists taken only the fertile land or best area into consideration for their calculation. There is also another possibility that as coastal Orissa possessed good river transactions, this share was available to everyone not because of the canal water but because of its river system.

Ever since the British arrived to India they documented and projected the events and programmes in such a way that will show them as benefactors who treated the welfare of their subjects as prime concern. Hence, in the colonial records, the depressed peasants did not exist. The truth was that after making all kinds of payments, and after managing cost of living the peasants hardly had earned any profit.[105] The increased amount of production that was discussed above did not make any difference in the lives of the peasants. They had to cop up with increased taxes and so on. When the yield was high, the peasants had to pay a high amount of tax according to the yield (as it was evident from different land revenue records in every year and in every settlement, land revenue was increased). Sometimes, there was over assessment of land tax and water tax also. Analysing the situation, Maddox, S.L., one of the Settlement Officers expressed his view in the *Final Report on the Survey and Settlement of the Province of Orissa, 1890-1900.* He viewed:

> In Orissa the normal rainfall being ample, the value of canal irrigation is exceptionally dependent on the character of the season. Cultivators frequently allege that they were in the first instances partly induced to take water leases by assurances of increased outrun, which have not been fulfilled; but in the opinion of many, and certainly in that of the Oriya peasant, the chief value of canal water lies not in any improvement which it may render possible in the outrun of an ordinary year, but in the protection which it affords against total or partial failure in years of drought.[106]

To conclude, there were no notable increase in production took place till 1939 which could be attributed to the canal irrigation system. The Orissa peasants used to consider the canal irrigation nothing more than an insurance against drought, as they used to go for its use only at the time of low rainfall.[107] Hence, if there was any increase in production not because of the canal irrigation but because of the climatic factors, nature of soil and use of conventional kind of water sources.

On the other hand, the common assumption of the colonialists that because of the canal irrigation the failure of crops did not take place is untenable under the above arguments of this chapter. Their assumptions are wrong. On the contrary, there were many examples to prove this notion created by the British is wrong. For instance, there was the failure of crops in Puri district in 1896 and again in 1918 due to shortage of rainfall.[108] Even prior to that, in 1887-88, there was a crop failure in the Puri district in general and Khorda division in particular.[109] Likewise, at Birso, Barbaria, Hosseinpore, and Debkumar regions of Balasore district witnessed a crop failure in 1888-89.[110] Next year too, the district saw another crop failure that struck the economy of the district.[111] The famine of 1888 and 1896 of Orissa were other insights into the very fact.[112] Until 1940s, there were several crop failure occurred in the state. Thus, it has been proved that the theory of development in the field of agriculture which was very strongly attributed to canal irrigation along with other agricultural policies that was founded by the so called colonialists cannot withstand to the data provided.

Notes

1. URL: https://aelarsen.wordpress.com/tag/enrico-lo-verso/; https://aelarsen.wordpress.com/tag/renzo-martinelli/ (Accessed on 06-06-2017).
2. *GAROD, 1873-1874,* p. 13.
3. *Ibid., 1874-1875,* p. 13.
4. *Ibid., 1873-1874,* p. 13.
5. *Ibid., 1874-1875,* p. 13.
6. *Ibid., 1875-1876,* p. 15.
7. *Ibid., 1876-1877,* p. 14.
8. *AGAROD, 1877-1878,* p. 30.
9. *Ibid.* p. 31.
10. *AGAROD, 1878-1879,* p. 39.

11. *Ibid.*, p. 31.
12. *GAROD, 1872-73*, p. 30.
13. *Ibid., 1873-1874*, p. 35.
14. *Ibid., 1875-1876*, pp. 2, 15.
15. *AGAROD, 1877-1878*, p. 8.
16. *Ibid., 1878-79*, p. 39.
17. *Ibid., 1883-84*, p. 36.
18. *Ibid., 1882-83*, p. 53.
19. *Ibid., 1883-84*, p. 36.
20. *Ibid., 1884-85*, p. 41.
21. *Ibid., 1885-86*, p. 44.
22. *Ibid., 1886-87*, p. 42.
23. *Ibid.*
24. *AGAROD, 1888-89*, p. 39.
25. *AGAROD, 1887-88*, p. 35.
26. *Report of the Irrigation Rates Revision Committee, op. cit.*, p. 12.
27. *AGROD, 1883-84*, p. 36.
28. *Ibid., 1883-84*, p. 37.
29. *Ibid.*
30. *AGAROD, 1888-89*, p. 39.
31. *Ibid., 1890-91*, p. 14.
32. *Ibid.*,
33. *Ibid., 1894-95*, p. 49.
34. *Ibid., 1897-98*, p. 39.
35. *Ibid., 1899-1900*, p. 31.
36. *Ibid., 1890-91*, p. 14.
37. *Ibid., 1899-1900*, p. 4.
38. *RABO, 1912-13*, p. 71.
39. *Ibid., 1915-16*, pp. 67-69.
40. *Ibid., 1917-18*, p. 74.
41. *Ibid., 1918-19*, p. 76.
42. *Ibid., 1919-20*, p. 61.
43. *Ibid., 1920-21*, p. 27.
44. *Bihar and Orissa in 1927-28*, Government of Bihar and Orissa, Patna, 1929, p. 83.
45. Jagamohan, R., *Bihar and Orissa in 1929-30*, Government of Bihar and Orissa, Patna, 1931, p. 93.

46. Mansfield, P.T. (1932). *Bihar and Orissa in 1930-31,* Government of Bihar and Orissa, Patna, p. XXXV.
47. Williams, R.A.E. (1933.) *Bihar and Orissa in 1931-32,* Government of Bihar and Orissa, Patna, p. 32.
48. Gupta, R.L. (1934). *Bihar and Orissa in 1932-33,* Government of Bihar and Orissa, Patna, p. 85.
49. Wilcock, J.S. (1935). *Bihar and Orissa in 1933-34,* Government of Bihar and Orissa, Patna, p. 91.
50. Solomon, S. (1937). *Bihar and Orissa in 1934-35,* Government of Bihar and Orissa, Patna, p. 122.
51. Mahapatra, Jadu Nath (1941). Orissa in 1936-37 to 1938-39, Government of Orissa, Cuttack, p. 109.
52. *Ibid.,* p. 132.
53. *SCRO, 1939-40,* p. 10.
54. *Ibid., 1941-42,* p. 6.
55. *Ibid., 1943-44,* p. 6.
56. *Ibid., 1944-45,* p. 6.
57. *Report on the Land Revenue Administration of the districts of North Orissa for the year 1946-47,* Government of Orissa, Cuttack, 1948, p. 3.
58. Mahapatra, Jadu Nath, *op. cit.,* p. 137.
59. *SCRO, 1941-42,* pp. 4-5.
60. See for example Bernard Darley, *op. cit.*
61. Mukherjee, Mridula (2005). *Colonizing Agriculture: The Myth of Punjab Exceptionalism,* Sage Publications India Private Limited, New Delhi.
62. For instance see, Macpherson, W.J. (2013). "Economic Development in India under the British Crown, 1858-1947", in A.J. Youngson (Ed.), *Economic Developments in the Long Run,* Routledge, London.
63. Maddox, L. (1900). *Final Report on the Survey and Settlement of the Province of Orissa, 1890 to 1900,* Vol.-I, Government of Bengal, Calcutta, p. 81.
64. *Ibid.,* p. 90.
65. *BODG: Puri,* p. 174.
66. *Ibid., Cuttack,* p. 91.
67. *Ibid.,* p. 116.
68. Mahapatra, Jadu Nath, *op. cit.,* p. 132.
69. URL: http://understandingsociety.blogspot.in/2009/05/longue-duree.html (Accessed on 8/6/2017); http://www.thehindu.com/

opinion/op-ed/what-is-longue-dure-in-historiography/article18159741.ece (Accessed on 8/6/2017)

70. Das, S. Binod (1976). "Orissa's Economy in the Nineteenth Century", *Social Scientist*, Vol. 4, No. 11, June, pp. 41-42.
71. Bandyopadhyay, Sekhar (2013). *From Plassey to Partition: A History of Modern India*, Orient Blackswan Private Limited, New Delhi, reprint p. 126.
72. Das, S. Binod, *op. cit.*, p. 32.
73. Chaudhury, Pradipta (1991). "Peasants and British Rule in Orissa", *Social Scientist*, Vol. 19, No. 8/9, Aug-Sep., p. 34.
74. Stone, Ian (1984). *Canal Irrigation in British India: Perspectives on Technological Change*, Cambridge University Press, Cambridge, pp. 8-9.
75. Mahapatra, Jadu Nath, *op. cit.*, pp. 143-145.
76. *Ibid.*, pp. 140-142.
77. *Ibid.*, p. 142.
78. *Ibid.*, p. 139.
79. Chaudhury, Pradipta, *op. cit.*, p. 36.
80. *Ibid.*
81. *AGAROD, 1899-1900*, p. 12.
82. Maddox, S.L., *op. cit.*, pp. 69-70.
83. *Balasore District Gazetteer Statistics, 1900-1901 to 1910-11*, Government of Bihar and Orissa, Patna, 1915, pp. 9-10.
84. *RABO, 1912-1913*, Patna, 1914, p. 53; *RABO, 1917-1918*, Patna, 1919, p. 52; *Bihar and Orissa in 1927-28*, Government of Bihar and Orissa, Patna, 1929, p. 88.
85. *Balasore District Gazetteer Statistics, 1900-1901 to 1910-11*, Government of Bihar and Orissa, Patna, 1915, p. 9; *Bihar and Orissa in 1927-28*, Government of Bihar and Orissa, Patna, 1929, p. 88.
86. *BODG: Puri*, p. 168.
87. Gupta, R.L., *op. cit.*, p. 89.
88. *BODG: Puri*, pp. 172-173.
89. *Bihar and Orissa in 1927-28*, Government of Bihar and Orissa, Patna, 1929, pp. 89-90.
90. Sahoo, Rajib Lochan (2004). *Agrarian Change and Peasant Unrest in Colonial India*, Orissa 1912-1939, Manak Publication, New Delhi, pp. 163-70.

91. Bhola, S.C. (1990). *British Economic Policy in Orissa (1905-1947),* Discovery Publishing House, New Delhi, pp. 167-68.
92. Mahapatra, Jadu Nath, *op. cit.*, p. 139.
93. *Agricultural Statistics of Orissa for 1939-40,* Government of Orissa, Cuttack, 1943, pp. 2-3; *SCRO, 1939-40,* pp. 8-9.
94. *SCRO, 1941-42,* pp. 6-7.
95. *Ibid., 1943-44,* pp. 6-7.
96. *Ibid., 1944-45,* pp. 6-7.
97. *Ibid., 1945-46,* pp. 6-7.
98. Chandra, B. (1999). *Essays on Colonialism,* Orient Blackswan Private Limited, New Delhi, pp. 127-128.
99. Maddox, S.L., *op. cit.*, p. 82.
100. *Ibid.*
101. *Ibid.*
102. *BODG: Puri,* pp. 176-77.
103. Mansfield, P.T., *op. cit.*, p. 93.
104. *BODG: Cuttack,* p. 86.
105. Behera, A.K., *op. cit.*
106. Maddox, S.L., *op. cit.*, p. 81.
107. Mahapatra, Jadu Nath, *op. cit.*, p. 132.
108. *BODG: Puri,* p. 168.
109. *AGAROD, 1887-88,* p. 34.
110. *Ibid.,1888-89,* p. 39.
111. *Ibid.,1889-90,* p. 9.
112. Das, Purna Chandra (1989). *The Economic History of Orissa in the 19th Century,* Commonwealth Publishers, New Delhi, pp. 105-6.

4
Canal Irrigation and Agrarian Market

> The Oriya cultivators are slow to appreciate the economic benefits of canal water, which is considered as nothing more than insurance in years of drought and an unnecessary luxury in years of copious and seasonal rainfall.
>
> —*Jadu Nath Mahapatra*[1]

The Orissa Canal Systems: A Prime Mover of Trade and Commerce

Pre-British Communication System

During the pre-British era, the people of Orissa used both land and River routes for the communication. River ways were important routes for both inland routes and communication. Bigger rivers like the Mahanadi, the Vaitarani, the Brahmani and the Subarnarekha and its tributaries were used for commercial purposes extensively. Country boats were made use of for large scale transport. Like the country boats, on the mainland, the Orissa people also used bullock carts for the transportation of commodities as well as people.[2] Various written records as well as archaeological evidences prove that there were good roads that connected to various parts of Orissa and it facilitated a very smooth running of inland trade.[3] Throughout 16th century, this kind of roads were seen in Orissa province.

British Period Communication System

With the advent of the British into Orissa state, they found that the communication and transportation system was by and large inadequate for the development of trade. From this realisation, they found the potentiality of the Rivers in Orissa and that resulted in the construction of various canals. This enabled them to carry out trade and commerce smoothly. This development, undoubtedly, helped Orissa to have a good transportation and communication system. From the bullock cart era to boat was a huge leap of development which cannot be denied.

However, for the British, the basic aim was the transportation of commodities from Orissa to Calcutta market. With the course of time, the new canal construction began and they began to use the canals for the desired objectives. However, records are scanty on the initial period of the development. The early evidence of canal passenger traffic shows that, the total passenger traffic were of mainly in the three important canals of coastal Orissa as shown in Table 4.1.

Table 4.1: Total Number of Passenger Traffic Over Three Major Canals

Years	*Kendrapara Canal*	*High Level Canal Range I*	*High Level Canal Range II*
1885-86	42,993	13,425	2,095
1886-87	43,798	7,542	5,976
1887-88	38,450	3,323	2,410
1888-89	51,117	6,638	4,077
1889-90	61,122	10,295	5,129

Source: *Annual General Administration Report for Orissa Division, for the year 1889-90*, Cuttack, 1890, p. 10.

The total passenger traffic for the year 1888-89 and 1889-90 including ports (with canals) was 1,34,463 and 1,46,277 respectively. Only in the Cuttack district, the principal routes by water were the Kendrapara Canal, the High Level Canal, the Taladanda Canal, and the River Mahanadi.[4] From Table 4.1, it is clear that from year to year the traffic increased. It was so because the rise of population and absence of railway system in Orissa.

From Cuttack to Kendrapara, there was a daily steamer service both for people and cargos. The daily steamer service, in fact, replaced the country boats that were used to transport commodities earlier.[5] Especially, in the Orissa Coast Canal, the traffic was high and on an average of 4,000 boats used to sail till 1920-21.[6] Government steamer continued to sail between Cuttack and Bhadrak.[7] The Taladanda canal used to provide an alternative route from Cuttack to Chanbali *via* Hansua creek. Likewise the Gobri canal remained a main route from Cuttack to Chanbali.[8] If it was so, therefore, there was a considerable number of boats must have been in use over the total Orissa canal circle.

On the way of canal communication both railway and scarcity of coal obstructed somewhat.[9] It has been proved from various administrative as well as yearly records. Even in the context of Puri district, its collector remarked that, the greater part of the traffic of the district went not by roads, but by the irrigation canals.[10] We have affluent amount of evidences to prove the both internal as well as external commodities transportation which has been mentioned in this chapter specifically.

With the improvement of road transportation and railway lines, canal transport system lost its past glory. Over a period of time, importance was given to the construction of roads For instance, in 1936 a Provincial Road Board was constituted, and it recommended six projects, out of which 5 were directly or indirectly within the geographical region of coastal Orissa.[11] But still canal transport was in use and its importance cannot be overlapped.

Pre-Railway Canal Trade

The very aim behind the construction of canals in Orissa, from the economic point of view, was the development of transport and communication.[12] With the construction of canals in Orissa, commodities primarily food items like rice, wheat, pulse, sugar etc., and non-food items like raw cotton, raw silk, tobacco, indigo, salt etc., began to be exported from Orissa to other places. The canal system not only helped in exporting various commodities but also in importing them.[13] Since Orissa was not connected with railways till 1898[14], the British extensively used the canal system for the inter-provincial and international trade and commerce. Unfortunately, we do not have sufficient data to show the extent of early trade and commerce through canal.

In Cuttack district, out of the total canal navigational routes, the primary canal routes were the Taladanda Canal, Kendrapara Canal and the Machgaon Canal.[15] In Balasore district, the High Level Canal and Orissa Coast Canal were the major routes which connected Balasore with Cuttack district indirectly.[16] Through the canals, commodities were transported to ports and from there to other provinces and countries. There is ample evidence that these routes were used for extensive trade.

In the year 1875-76 alone, over the High Level Canal, an average of 220 government and 1,806 private boats sailed, carrying cargos worth about Rs. 14,775 and Rs. 3,57,733 for the Government and the private trade respectively. Similarly, on the Kendrapara Canal, on an average around 295 government traffic boats and 3,857 private traffic boats sailed in the same year. The value of cargo in the government sector was Rs. 15,364 and Rs. 33,08,702 in the private trade. The Taladanda Canal had the highest traffic by the Government among all other canals in this year and the private traffic had registered low in this sector. While there were 329 government traffic boats and the private traffic boats were 729. The value of cargos in the government sector was Rs. 2,621, while the value was Rs. 1,46,418 for the private cargo.[17] One of the earliest evidence of commodities transportation through the Coast Canal was found in the *Annual General Report of Orissa Division for the year 1889-90*. The district collector stated in the report that the seaborne trade declined by 1889-

90, partially because of the completion of the construction of the Coast Canal.[18] During 1889-90, the total value commodities carried through the Coast Canal was Rs. 5,74,531 and the profit they got was Rs. 25,435. The traded commodities were mainly grain, oilseeds, salt, building materials, cotton, timber etc.[19] by 1890-91, the value of these commodities increased to Rs. 5,77,448 and total income from this trade was Rs. 26,002.[20] This indicates the high demand and significant role of canal in trade and commerce.

Post-Railway Canal Trade

The post-1897-98 period saw a new phase of trade and commerce with the introduction of railways in Orissa. And soon it became an alternative for the Canal system in Orissa. During 1897-98 total import to Orissa through canals was 2,37,153 maunds whereas through railway it was 2,98,503 maunds. Similarly during the next year (for 1898-99), the total import through Canals was 2,97,218 maunds and by rail it was almost tripled – 6,29,948 maunds. Gradually, the railways took over the major share of the transport and trade and as a result the share of canals declined to 2,00,321maunds, while the share of the railways increased to 9,80,267 maunds by next year.[21] Table 4.2 shows the variation in the trade share of canal system and the railways.

Table 4.2: Total Import of Commodities through Canal and Railway

(*in Maunds*)

	Import (in Maunds)		
Years	*Canal*	*Railway*	*Total*
1897-98	2,37,153	2,98,503	5,35,656
1898-99	2,97,218	6,29,943	9,27,161
1899-1900	2,00,321	9,80,267	11,8U,588

Source: *Annual General Administration Report of the Orissa Division, for the year 1899-1900*, Cuttack, 1900, p. 11.

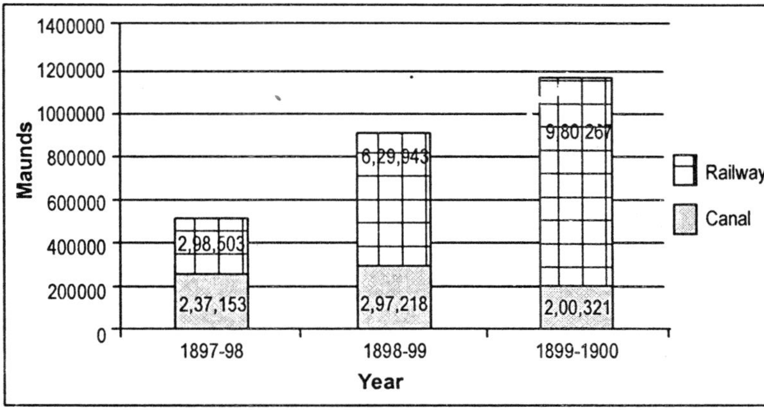

Fig. 4.1: Total Import of Commodities through Canal and Railway from 1897-98 to 1899-1900 (in maunds).

From Fig. 4.1, it is clear that the share of trade and trasport with railways went up year by year and coresspondigly, the demand for canal communication went downwards. This was due to the railway transportation was simpler and easier than the canal transportation. Commodities found their way to Orissa from Bengal province an easier way. Though, the share of canal transport had gone down, still the importance for trade and commerce through this channel was not to be ignored.

Unsurprisingly, even in the export trade, the importance of Orissa canals gradually declined. During 1897-98, the total amount of exported commodities through canal was 11,98,028 maunds; for the railways the share was 3,31,732 maunds. However, the very next year the canal trade had a higher share of 6,65,886 maunds commodities transferred, but for the railways, the amount was 1,52,300 maunds. Followed by this, during 1899-1900, the share of railway export increased to 17,85,315 maunds and through canal only 4,25,649 maunds amount of commodities transferred.[22] Fig. 4.2 gives the account of the export share of the canal system and the railways.

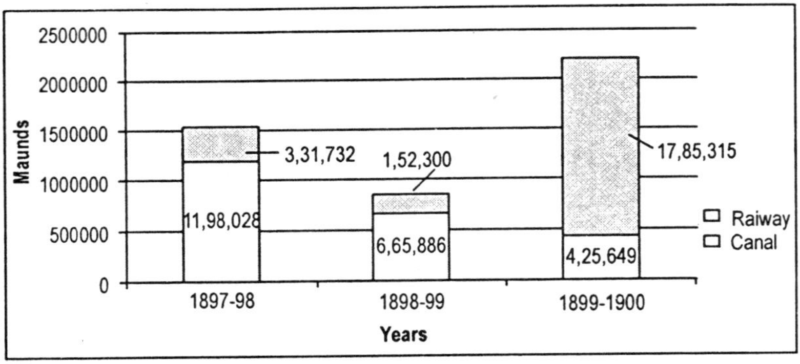

Fig. 4.2: Export of Commodities through Railway and Canal from 1897-98 to 1899-1900 (in maunds).

But in the case of exports, the first two years, the share of canal transportation was higher than railways. It was so because the railways were just got introduced and commodity transportation by the railways was unfamiliar to the people of Orissa. Except this, no other explanation is avaiable. So, roughly speaking, Canal's importance was still considerable.

By the year 1915-16, the total length of navigational canals was 204¾ miles. Over the canal system during the year 1915-16 around 4,03,972 tons of commodities were transported by boats and the estimated value was around Rs. 1,05,96,167. But taking an average for the three preceding years (1912-13, 1913-14 and 1914-15), 3,81,463 tons of commodities were transported over the same lengths of canal. The estimated value of the transferred commodities was around Rs. 1,24,81,516, which was little more than that of the estimated value of the year 1915-16.[23] Likewise, a complete traffic statement on the navigable canals for the year 1917-18 showed by the same year around 4,51,329 tons of commodities were transferred over the Orissa canal system whose total length was the same like 204¾ miles, excluding the Orissa Coast canal. The estimated value of those carried commodities was Rs. 1,05,29,326. In the particular context over the Orissa Coast canal (total length of the navigable canal was 95½ miles) around 35,070 tons of commodities were transported whose estimated coast was Rs. 7,11,103.[24] The average trasportation over the Orissa canal circle in the three preceding years (1914-15, 1915-16 and 1916-17) was around 3,99,784 tons and estimated cost was Rs. 1,04,44,738.[25] This rhythm of transportation remained intact because of the atomsphere of the First World War. Around 4,49,965 tons of commodities were transported over Orissa canal circle with an estimated value of around Rs. 1,15,13,902, whereas over the Orissa Coast canal 29,617 tons of commodities were transferred valuing about Rs. 6,38,324.[26] In 1918-19, the total amount of commodities carried on canals was little less but value was somehow higher. On the other hand, in the case of the Orissa Coast canal both the amount of transferred commodities as well as its estimated value declined to some extent comparing to preceding years. An average of transported commodities in the context of the Orissa canal circle for the last three years (1915-16, 1916-17 and 1917-18) was around 4,21,182 tons with an estimated value of Rs. 1,07,28,793. And the average estimated value of commodities for the last three years for the Orissa Coast canal was around Rs. 6,43,598.[27] The pace of transportation declined by next year (1919-20) to 3,61,830 tons of commodities, and the estimated value was around Rs. 1,03,52,951 in the context of Orissa Canal circle. But by the year, the toatl length of navigable canal under Orissa Canal Circle was 205¼ miles as there was one mile additional extension of canal system in the old existed system. On the other hand under the Orissa Coast canal system, the amount of transferred commodities increased too much and reached to 1,21,414 tons, whose estimated value was around Rs. 8,86,116.[28]

But regarding the unprecedented rise of trade in the context of Orissa Coast Canal and drastic decline in the trade in the case of Orissa Canal circle, no specific reason had been mentioned. But all of a sudden export through the canal increased on account of better harvests.[29] In Orissa, the Orissa Coast Canal possesed its own importance. Every year an average of some 4,000 boats used the canal.

The canal used to provide inland route from Cuttack to Calcutta.[30] It is only an example in relation to the Orissa Coast Canal. If it was so then regarding the Orissa Canal circle the transaction must have been large.

Out of all the three coastal districts of Orissa, the trade of Puri was of far less importance than that of Cuttack or Balasore. The principal articles of export was rice or paddy.[31] Rice used to be exported to different provinces. In this regard, the Orissa canal system played a very important role. For the years 1926-27, 1927-28 and 1928-29, the average transferred commodities amount was around 4,18,980 tons.[32] In 1929-30, around 3,79,952 tons of commodities were transferred through the Orissa Canal system.

During 1931-32, the total transported commodities amount was 3,34,000 tons. Around 3,75,000 tons of commodities were transferred through Orissa Canal system during the year 1932-33.[33] Since the two consecutive years, Orissa's trade and commerce was in a general depression mode.[34] Later on the tempo of trade and commerce became slow and the trend continued till 1946-47. This was mostly for the expansion of railway networks to major resourceful areas. To conclude the section, the importance of canal system of Orissa lies in the fact that the colonialist benefited from it enormousely because the high level trade and commerce by the way of transfer of commodities from one place to another was carried by the British only. This is very easy claim that Oriya peasants were not involved in this large scale transportation or commercial activities as they were poor and did not have capacity to continue with the British.

Changing Nature of Agrarian Market in Coastal Orissa

Local Markets in the Pre-British Period

Earlier days, markets were widespread and these were knows as *hats* (local markets). *Hats* used to hold twice in a week in villages. These were generally consisted of a group of rickety stalls huddled together in a convenient mango tope, for the use of it the stall-keepers and vendors had to pay fees in cash or kind to the owner. In the larger *hats,* the general attendance of villagers was above thousand. These markets were used by the farmers in the villages to trade of their surplus agricultural produces and other local produces and used to purchase cotton, ornaments, metal utensils, spices, kerosene oil, and several other articles. Barter system was practiced in many cases.[35] The most important factor here is that the surplus production was always consumed by local people within whom the spirit of indigenous market system was alive.

Sometimes, the *hats* used to arrange near to a temple. All the trade items used to come from near villages, situated in and around the temple.[36] Farmers mostly traded the subsistence crops. These kinds of *hats* might have been organised near the temple in order to cater the needs of pilgrims who came to visit the temple places from distant places. The *hats* system, in short, provided an equal opportunity for the producers to trade their excess produce in order to buy other products. Similarly, it also used to allow every seller to accumulate money which they used to invest during the time of cultivation. Sometimes, the sellers used to get higher prices for their selling commodities by selling commodities to pilgrims.[37]

Items in the Local Markets

The local *hats* were otherwise called *Pattanas*. Those local towns enjoyed commercial prosperity on account of chief transport.[38] Agriculture and different industries enabled the Orissa merchants to trade with different kinds of natural items as well as artificial items. Agricultural produce like rice, wheat, barley, salt, incense, elephants, conch shell, stone, iron products, timber items were the main items of trade. Along with these items, different kinds of perfumes, pottery items, gold items and garment items were exhibited and people used to buy from these from local *hats* or *pattanas.*[39] It was basically meant for the consumption of that locality. Similarly, there were bigger local markets, little bit bigger *hats,* and they used to sell import items such as pearl, silver items, silk items, and spices from different countries or states.

Medium of Exchange

In those local *hats* most of the items were exchanged through barter system.[40] This system of exchange was the main order of those days. But many other items were exchanged by *madha,* a piece of gold, *pana,* a currency, *rupya,* a piece of silver and several others were used. Along with that *cowrie shells* also was a kind of currency which was frequently used by people as the medium of exchange.[41] Interestingly, the ban on the usage of *the Cowrie shells* as currency was one of the reasons for the outbreak of the Paik rebellion of 1817 in Orissa. This ban was imposed in November 1804. It had its rate of exchange with the silver coins.[42] Within which existed *Builion,* an indigenous currency was also in use, which was in the form of various metals (hiranya of records).[43]

Market Places

Many places developed as business centres. Average market places emerged basically on the banks of different rivers. Such were Choudwar, on the Mahanadi-Birupa River, Viraja on the bank of Vaitarani and Guhadevpatak on the bank of river Vaitarani near Jajpur.[44] Sanchataka, Amarataksaka and Sagada were other market places in the Jajpur and Cuttack region. Murasima Pattana, Saumyapura, Matruchandrapataka, Sarabhapura, Sripura, Kalingapura and so on were also the important towns of Orissa.[45]

Markets after Canal Construction

With the opening of canals and railways, India turned into a mere market for the British manufactured commodities, and also served as a source of agricultural raw materials.[46] Orissa was not an exception to this. With the introduction of extensive canal system and later on railways and roads in Orissa, foreign commodities began to pour to the markets in the state.[47] A large number of foreign commodities including gunny bags, cloth, gram[48], European commodities, coal, coke, kerosene oil, salt, brass, hardware, and twist, and other miscellaneous articles became common during those days.[49] In a way, it destroyed the local markets by replacing the local produce to foreign commodities. It was a big loss for the Orissa peasants. First of all, their income had been reduced. Along with foreign commodities, commercialized crops also became the main selling items of those markets. Those newly imported foreign commodities began to be sold at the fixed prices which was determined or fixed by them. This was a major point where the locals lost their control over their market and so the prospects of trade and commerce.

On the other hand because of the opening of canals, agricultural products from the Coastal Orissa found their way to Madras, Central Provinces and several other places.[50] All the three districts (Balasore, Cuttack and Puri) were chief exporters of the both food and non-food crops to Calcutta, Central Provinces and Madras, as these provinces had good canal and River system that connected to the ports. This made the transportation easier than any other parts of India. As a result of heavy demand for commodities for trade, often prices shot up in the districts and this led to artificial shortage of food grains. For example, in 1877, due to the high transportation of rice to Madras, paddy prices rose up in the districts of Puri and Cuttack. The Khorda market, Jajpore Road Town and Kendrapara also witnessed such price hike. However, Balasore district was not affected in this regard.[51] In 1878, the prices touched nearly three times higher than what it used to be.[52] This resulted in the scarcity of food grains. It became such an issue that people complained to District Collector to take steps to stop excess transportation in Cuttack district.[53] The prices used to fluctuate from time to time depending upon the rate of transportation.

With the advent of the British, when trade became a huge enterprise, a new class of people emerged with that and they dominated the Orissa markets. It should be mentioned here that the chief traders or merchants were outsiders or foreigners. From the local ignorant peasants they used to purchase different commodities by paying a very minimum rate from which no profit could be exacted after paying all kinds of rents or invests and taxes. For instance, the rice merchants principally were Muhammadans from Bombay, the cloth merchants were Marwaris from Marwar region of Rajasthan, the hide dealers Kabulis were from Afghanistan. The major portion of local and general trade and commerce was in the hands of outsiders, which replaced Orissa's local traders.[54] A large number of Telugu and Marwari merchants took up their quarters in the town of Balasore.[55] Of course, the intermittent famine that was experienced in other parts of the country was responsible for this. For example, the famine of Madras led them to reach places like Orissa to fetch rice and such other food grains as there was a heavy demand for this.[56]

As a result of expansion of trade, new principal markets emerged nearer to canal periphery. Kantilow, Badyaswar, Rahama, Alba, Aul, Jajpur Road town, Kendrapara town and so on were the best examples of new emerged markets. Besides those markets, there were also minor marts held every week throughout the Cuttack district.[57]

Overall it can be said that the canal changed whole indigenous market system where there was very minimum chance for the poor peasants to earn profit out of market system. In the new market, peasants lost their independency as all the marketed items were mainly of British origin.

SUFFERINGS OF THE PEASANTRY UNDER THE CANAL IRRIGATION SYSTEM

Like all other parts of colonial India, the peasants of Orissa were also got affected by the *reforms* introduced by the British. The newly devised canal irrigation impacted the Orissa peasants in many ways: there were direct implications as well as indirect ones. The projects introduced by the British were highly exploitative and the peasants in Orissa suffered enormously with the economic policies of the British. In the name of providing service to them, the Britsh were making profits out of these so-called services. So let us have a look at this in detail.

The foremost implication in relation to canal irrigation was that, it took away the self-depended nature of the Oriya peasants; they had been carrying out the agricutural actvities depedning on rains and when that source was not available, they made use of the indigenous water sources the community maintained them as well. This built up a feeling of ownership too. And the farming was an independent actvity as they need not depend on the prescribed timing or follow the calendar of the irrigation facilities from the canal irrigation. Everybody used to irrigate according to the need of water to their agricultural land. The canal system changed everything drastically including the rythm of the farming which was followed for centuries. The irrigational facilities were completely monoplised by the British and they dictated the terms and conditions. The cultivators did not have any say in the matter. New bureaucrats began to dictate everything (tax pattern, canal operation, technical designs, distributions, abolition of rights of canal). To avail canal water, they have to apply in a prescirbed application form supplied by the concerned authorities and the same to be submitted to the Supertending Engineer.[58] The dates of water release in order to irrigate to their agricultural land for each season was always fixed by the colonialists. Normally, an year was divided into three seasons for irrigation purpose: hot weather from March to June; *kharif*, from June to October and *rabi*, from November to March.[59] Simultaniously, a lease or permission was granted for this; but, the sanctioned lease used to last for that particular season only.[60] The farmers had to repeat the exercise in every season. Up on the lease application, the executive engineer used to make a field survey and assess the cultivator's land. After assessing the land one possessed, he used to fix water rate for the particular land. Normally, the peasants used to agree with the water rate fixed by the authority without questioning it.[61] A separate administration unit was set up to look after the affairs of the canal administration. This was under the supervision of Public Works Department, which included few expert engineers.[62] Once the water tax had been fixed, the farmers were required to pay the tax irrespective of the fact that wheather they required water or not for the season. Of course in this matter, a few local elements were also indulged.[63] Already different land laws, which were implemented over a period of time, impoverished the Orissa peasants considerably. In addition to this, local elements (*zamindars*) also palyed a havoc on their lives. However, their presence in this matter made all the things ravish. By different laws, their position got established very strongly, which allowed them to intervene in the economic matter of the peasants.

The loss of traditional water bodies became another major crisis for the poor peasants, which was not felt earlier but later on. With the propagation of canal system throughout the coastal Orissa, the British did not pay any attention to the indigenous kinds of irrigational sources, as these were not profitable from economic point of view. With the due course of time, the number of indeginous irrigational sources declined and these were ceased to act as alternative water sources. However, it was not to deny the fact here that some of the British officials had a good understanding about the traditional water sources and it had aready stated that the Indian Famine Commission of 1901, which was constituted to look into the great famine of 1898 which stressed on the necessity of irrigation system, which included both traditional and canal irrigation. Even private enterprisers were invited in this endeavour.[64] However, as far as the revival of the traditional water sources were concerned, nothing happened beyond the recommendations. Indigenous irrigation systems started declining gradually. The consequences of the corrotion of these bodies were huge; the adverse effects are apparent even today.

Yet, another adverse impact of the British intervenion in the agriculture sector was on the subsistence crops. The introduction of commercial crops affected the food security of the state adversly. Earlier Orissa peasants used to produce only subsistence crops, which were consumed by the local people. This was evident from the products that were marked those days. All those crops that were marketed in those local areas were mainly locally produced.[65] The British popularised the potential of commercial crops along with the newly introduced canal irrigation system. Initially, for an incentive for the cultivation of commercial crops, the colonialists reduced the water rate.[66] Like the loss of independency on irrigation, the farmers lost control over the production—this time it was about what to produce and for whom. Over a period of time, cultivation of commercial crops picked up slowly and steadily. Now, even the prices of those crops and its transportation to different markets came under the British control. And the Orissa peasants became just producers of those crops which was dictated by somebody else; the alienation became complete.

In addition to this, the amount of water tax was also high. Initially, when the East India and Canal Company commenced their operations, there was no specific rule for levy of water rates. The Directors of the company prepared to leave the matter to be settled while the work was in progress. The first Act related to irrigation was was No. VIII of 1867 of Bengal Council. Section 2 of this Act empowered to framing regulations for levy of water rates. It was decided to sell water by volume and by the area irrigated. Rs. 2.50 per acre for 50 acres and above of the area irrigated and Rs. 5.00 per acre below 10 acres of the area irrigated was fixed.[67]

But water was not sold by volume. In 1869, Act VI laid a new set of regulations in this regard. Now importance was given for the sales by volume. One rupee was fixed upon per 1,000 cubic yards between the period 15th January and the 31st October. And it was increased to Rs. 1.50 per 1,000 cubic yards during the rest of the year. Along with that rate, the area was also determined. Rs. 6 per acre for sugarcane crop; Rs. 5 per acre for any crop other than sugarcane; Rs. 3 per crop for any single crop not remaining more than 6 months on the ground was fixed.[68]

The idea of selling water by volume was replaced by system of lease from 1872 onwards. According to the new regulation, water rates were reduced to some extent. One rupee was fixed per acre on the leases which were executed before the 1st May of the year and Rs. 1.50 per acre on the leases after the 1st May of that year. But pre payment of the half of the rate was compulsory.[69]

The new Bengal Irrigation Act of 1880, laid new rules for this. Under that Rs. 1.50 per acre for flow of irrigation and Rs. 1.00 per acre for lift, when irrigable area of the rice lands of a village was leased and when the lease was for a term of years. Subsequently, this was changed into the term of 5 years. For lease of a less area than the above or for shorter periods, a rate of Rs. 3 per acre was required.[70]

Those rates continued till 1892, then few changes were made in this regard. Low land which did not ordinarily benefit by canal irrigation were assessed at Rs. 0.50 per acre. Very low lands were exempted from assessment, as those kind never required irrigation. Rs. 2 per acre was assessed on the applications that were made after 1st September.[71]

Further few more changes were brought in the old pattern in 1895. Rs. 1.50 was fixed per acre (*Mana was called in Odia language)* per season for a term of 7 years. In the low lying lands not requiring canal water in normal years was fixed at the rate of Re. 0.50 per acre per season. Unauthorised use of canal water was fixed at Rs. 5 per acre. Rs. 3 per acre was fixed for the one year leased lands. Similarly, rates were fixed for the lands where water was supplied otherwise than on a lease. Only to water *khariff* crop between 16th June and 30th November was fixed at the rate of Rs. 3 per acre. For Dalua paddy (summer rice) Rs. 1.50 per acre was fixed. Irrigation of cotton, tobacco, *Haldi*, ginger, wheat, vegetable, indigo and other garden products were charged at Rs. 1.50 per acre, whereas Re. 1 was charged on linseeds, oil-seeds and pulses crops. For sugarcane Rs. 5 was charged.[72]

But the water rate was increased from Rs. 1.50 to Rs. 1.75 in 1903.[73] From that amount it was again increased to Rs. 2 in 1912.[74] Later it increased to Rs. 3 and only was reduced by 25 per cent in 1938.[75] In 1939, the rates were further reduced due to the economic depression. The rate that was fixed in 1939 remained intact till independence.[76] From the very above discussion it is clear that peasants did not have a free hand either in the mattters of irrigation or in the matters of selecting the crops. The heavy burden of tax (irrigational tax and land tax) made them poorer.

In addition to the additional tax burden, the long term lease was also another matter of discontent. *Utkal Dipika*, an Odia newspaper, brought up the dissatisfaction of the farmers on this issue in its report. It stated that the farmers were unhappy about the long term agreement for canal water. Another reason being the very higher and very lower agricultural lands were not profited by the canal water. And thirdly, even after making payments peasants did not get water for their land. The authorities for the releasing of water to land were sometimes made to be pleased by the the poor peasants, which was an illigal as well as an extra burden for the peasants. Sometimes, people repeatedly visited officers for canal water. Even frequently the officers used to release water less than the prescribed quantity, which was inadequate. However, the farmers mostly kept quiet fearing repercussions.[77] In short, the conditions set out by the newly introduced canal system was not in favour of the poor farmers. On the other hand, both water ways (River and canal systems) and land routes helped the colonialists to trade commodities, especially foreign commodities enormousely. As a result, foreign commodities found their way to different markets throughout coastal Orissa. Needless to say that it affected the traditional industries like weaving and spinning, which also disturbed a large number of peasants adversly. These traditional industries provided an additional income to the farmers in Orissa. Thousands of peasants lost another source of livelihood due to the decline of traditional industries. It resulted in incidence of extreme poverty.

Land revenue policies left the Orissa peasants at the mercy of the British officers. High assesment of land revenue burdened the farmers severely. In the *zamindari* areas, the assessment was half of the total production.[78] With this, the addition of water tax made them to suffer a lot. As stated earlier, initially the water tax was made low to encourge the cultivation of commercial crops. Gradually, they increased the rate with the sole intension of maximising their revenue. The high water tax and the poor rainfall together push the peasants into debt trap. In order to save their crops, the peasants were bound to give the decided tax amount. But whole together it broke the backbone of the Orissa peasants and impoverished them completely.[79]

All the way, the Orissa peasants agitated with the cruel nature of the British. It resulted into peasants revolts in Orissa. The Kanika revolt 1921-22 of Orissa was one such example where only peasants went against their lords taking the issue of agrarian problems where the problem of taxation was one among their cause of their discontent. There are references about this revolt in contemporary literature in the state. One of the descriptions of the revolt in the popular literature depicted as a journal titled *krushak*, where a wrightup was prepared by Sachi Routroy, an eminent Odia Marxist revolutionary, in 1938. It described the tempo of revolt against the exploitation: (only few stanzas are qouted)

... Let the Earth tremble under the weight of your feet
You, Red soldiers, should march forward with the speed of cyclone
and
Surround the camp of the enemy. March on ...
See how the Raja and the government have combined
And are hunting human beings
The butcher is throttling men
Hold fast your weapon.
Destroy the foreign rule, that is at the root of all exploitation
Its soldiers and army are devastating your land ...
Dance today in the orgy of blood
Death will bring your deliverance

The bondage or slavery round your neck would be turn;
Your victory is certain......
The dance of exploitation is going on today
The life of human being has become marketable commodity;
Seeing all these you red soilders, unfurl your red banner....
Establish the reign of labour in the world,
That is your Konark, that is your Taj,
Shake off your fear, shake off your shame today
I bow down at your feet."[80]

CONCLUSION

From 1803, Coastal Orissa entered into a new phase of history as it entered into the colonial era from the Bhonsle branch of the Maratha rule. Interventions in every matter of coastal Orissa by the colonialists became order of those days. At that time, coastal colonial Orissa comprised of three districts such as, Balasore, Cuttack and Puri districts. The coastal belt was fertile one, due to the flowing of many major rivers. However, its geography was very much attractive.

Its main way of sustenance was agriculture. In the pre-colonial era, coastal Orissa peasants developed their own indigenous system of irrigation in order to manage agricultural activities. Local elements were the one, whose attention was always on agriculture's development. Financial assistance used to come for the development of different kinds of traditional irrigation sources. People were free to irrigate their agricultural land; in the sense that whenever they required water, they used to irrigate their land. They were independent from irrigation point of view. With the introduction of canal irrigation by the British, the use of different traditional water sources came down along with its number. In addition, the local people were no more responsible for the maintenances of traditional water resources as they had no power any more. All the power was retained with the British. The indifference attitude of the British towards the water sources brought their demise, as they felt the fact that those traditional water sources were not remunerative for them. No more maintenance to those traditional water sources led the demise of those.

With the objective of the accumulation of money and with an intention to bring stability of income by different ways, the British introduced the canal irrigation. This was actually their internal intentions whereas, to save the land from the disastrous famine and flood were the explicit causes behind the introduction of canal irrigation. The process of canal construction started mainly from 1869-70 onwards. Nevertheless, the process of extension was very low. In the matter of slow extension, rainfall and flood obstructed them. Side by side the introduction of railway in 1897-98 in Coastal Orissa gave fatal struck to the high progress of canal extension. Orissa but the accusation made by the British was that the Oriya peasants were ignorant and apathetic to avail any kind of scientific development. However, until 1918-19, canals extension was in a sound pace. Nevertheless, from 1920s, the canal extension was slow owing to the lack of British interest. In their thought, the Orissa canal project was not remunerative anymore as railway extension was already available in Coastal Orissa. Hereafter, the colonialists gave attention to only channels or branch canals. But till even the last movement of independence they continued the extension.

The expansion of canal irrigation went in full swing until 1918-19, but after it continued but it was slow. Their canal expansion was slow due to the fact that at the time of low rainfall peasants used to move for canal irrigation. The initial claim of the imperialists that the development of agriculture took place because of canal has been proved to be a myth as it was disclosed by the poor peasants that in real sense there was no expansion of cultivation except the reclamations of few sandy areas, took place. The peasants of Orissa used to consider the canal irrigation nothing beyond an insurance against the years of low rainfall. The canal irrigation changed the cropping pattern of Orissa under which the cultivation of commercial crops became an order in the colonial period. For their need, the colonialists consistently attempted to divert the peasants towards the cultivation of commercial crops by different ways, such as, by the application of experiments over different commercial crops by agricultural farms and reducing water tax. On the other hand, the additional burden of water tax along with the heavy land tax in cash payment system pushed the poor peasants all of a sudden to a confusing place. To manage the payment, poor peasants moved for the cultivation of commercial crops. Now, the nature of production changed from subsistence to commercial. Peasants produced no more for themselves only, but side by side, they produced for the markets demand and for the colonialists. Similarly, the claim of the colonialists that canal irrigation shut down the concept of failure of crops once again has been proved a vague one, as there were many instances of the failures of crops in colonial coastal Orissa with the presence of canal irrigation.

Further, with the introduction of the canal irrigation, communication and goods transfer became easier from one place to another. Now, Coastal Orissa was opened to the outside market and according to the demand of outside markets the rhythm of transfer of goods used to fluctuate. A new problem of scarcity of food grains was seen because the heavy transfer of food grains to other provinces.

Poor peasants of Coastal Colonial Orissa became a mere follower of the British commands in the irrigation sector. The introduction of the canal irrigation made the colonialists a dictator in this regard. Freedom of the poor peasants was no more as they were all regulated by the colonialist's direction in the matter of the amount of tax fixation, the day, date, and time of water release and overall water distribution, everything was decided by them only. On the other hand, high demand of water tax made the peasants unhappy. Even after paying, the fixed water tax peasants sometimes failed to receive water. Along with that, there was no real sense value in the case of very high lands and very low lands and new reclamations of land for cultivation, which could be attributed to the canal irrigation. So, all the ways, the peasants of colonial Coastal Orissa were dissatisfied.

With the extension of canal system in Coastal Orissa, the features of indigenous market system declined. Now many new markets emerged where the majority of high standard merchants were from out sides or the white people. For which the scope of income for Coastal Orissa peasants declined to minimum. Moreover, the goods, which were generally imported from outside, replaced the indigenous goods, for which the income of the poor peasants declined to certain extent. Here also in market system, poor people had problem because of canal system.

References

1. Mahapatra, Jadu Nath (1941). *Orissa in 1936-37 to 1938-39*, Government of Orissa, Cuttack p. 132.
2. Panda, Harihar (2014). *History of Odisha*, Cuttack: Kitab Mahal, pp. 149-151.
3. Mishra, D.B. (2011). *Concise History of Orissa*, Cuttack: Kalyani Publishers, pp. 289-90.
4. *AGAROD, 1889-90*, pp. 09-10.
5. *RABO, 1915-16*, pp. 68-69.
6. Owen, G.E. (1922). *Bihar and Orissa in 1921*, Government of Bihar and Orissa, Patna, p. 64.
7. *AGROD, 1882-83*, p. 56.
8. Maddox, S.L. (1900). *Final Report on the Survey and Settlement of the Province of Orissa, 1890 to 1900*, Vol. I, Government of Bengal, Calcutta, p. 23.
9. *Bihar and Orissa in 1927-28,* Government of Bihar and Orissa, Patna, 1929, p. 83; *RABO, 1918-1919*, p. 77.
10. *AGROD, 1878-79*, p. 40.
11. Mahapatra, Jadu Nath, *op. cit.*, 1941, p. 134.
12. *AGAROD, 1874-1875*, p. 8.
13. *Ibid., 1899-1900*, pp. 11-12
14. *Ibid.*, pp. 11.
15. *Ibid., 1889-90*, p. 9.
16. *Ibid.*, p. 10; Ganeswar Nayak, "The Coast Canal in Orissa during the Colonial Era", *Orissa Review*, May-June-2010, p. 67.
17. Das, Purna Chandra (1989). *The Economic History of Orissa in the 19th Century*, New Delhi: Commonwealth Publishers, p. 117.

18. *AGAROD, 1889-90*, p. 9.
19. *Ibid.*, p. 37.
20. *Ibid., 1890-91*, p. 31.
21. *Ibid., 1899-1900*, p. 11.
22. *Ibid., 1899-1900*, p. 12.
23. *RABO, 1915-1916*, p. 68.
24. *Ibid., 1917-1918*, p. 73.
25. *Ibid.*,
26. *Ibid., 1918-1919*, p. 75.
27. *Ibid.*,
28. *Ibid., 1919-1920*, p. 62.
29. *Ibid., 1920-1921*, p. 27.
30. Owen, G.E., *op. cit.*, p. 64.
31. *BODG: Puri*, p. 212.
32. Jagamohan, J. (1931). *Bihar and Orissa in 1929-30,* Government of Bihar and Orissa, Patna, p. 93.
33. Gupta, R.L. (1934). *Bihar and Orissa in 1932-33*, Government of Bihar and Orissa, Patna, p. 85.
34. Wilcock, J.S. (1935). *Bihar and Orissa in 1933-34,* Government of Bihar and Orissa, Patna, p. 91.
35. *BODG: Puri*, p. 213.
36. Panda, Harihar. *op. cit.*, p. 147.
37. *Ibid.*
38. Mishra, D.B. *op. cit.*, p. 290.
39. Panda, Harihar. *op. cit.*, p. 151.
40. *BODG: Puri*, p. 213.
41. Panda, Harihar. *op. cit.*, p. 152.
42. *Ibid.* pp. 236-237.
43. Mishra, D.B. *op. cit.*, p. 290.
44. Panda, Harihar. *op. cit.*, p. 149.
45. Mishra, D.B. *op. cit.*, p. 290.
46. Sekhar, Bandyopadhyay (2013). *From Plassey to Partition: A History of Modern India*, Orient Blackswan Private Limited, reprint, p. 122.
47. Bhola, S.C. (1990). *British Economic Policy in Orissa,* New Delhi: Discovery Publishing House, p. 145.
48. *AGAROD, 1876-77*, p. 10.
49. *AGAROD, 1899-1900*, p. 13.
50. *Ibid., 1876-77*, p. 6.

51. *Ibid.*, p. 7.
52. *Ibid., 1877-78*, p. 15.
53. *Ibid.*, p. 16.
54. Bhola, S.C. *op. cit.*, p. 145.
55. *AGAROD, 1876-77*, p. 8.
56. *Ibid.*, p. 4.
57. *Ibid., 1889-90*, p. 10.
58. *BODG: Puri*, p. 114.
59. *Ibid.*
60. *Ibid.*
61. *Ibid.*
62. Mahapatra, Jadu Nath (1941). *op. cit.*, p. 130; *BODG: Cuttack*, pp. 113-14.
63. *BODG: Cuttack*, p. 115.
64. *Report on the Indian Famine Commission, 1901, and Papers Relating Thereto*, Darling & Son Ltd., London, 1901, p. 112.
65. Panda, Harihar, *op. cit.*, p. 151.
66. Mahapatra, Jadu Nath, *op. cit.*, p. 139.
67. *Report of the Irrigation Rates Revision Committee*, Government of Orissa, 1967, p. 12.
68. *Ibid.* p. 13.
69. *Ibid.*
70. *Ibid.*
71. *Ibid.*
72. *Ibid.*
73. Das, Purna Chandra, *op. cit.*, p. 119.
74. Samal, J.K. (1990). *Economic History of Orissa, 1866-1912*, New Delhi: Mittal Publications, p. 99.
75. Samal, J.K. (1993). *Agrarian History of Orissa under the British Rule*, New Delhi: Kanishka Publishers, p. 199.
76. *Report of the Irrigation Rates Revision Committee, op. cit.*, p. 13.
77. Ray, Pratap Kumar (2010). *Kendrapara Zilla Itihasa*, second part, Bhubaneswar: Swastik Publication, pp. 107-108.
78. Mahapatra, Jadu Nath, *op. cit.*, p. 114.
79. Bhola, S.C., p. 144.
80. *The Krushak Song*, 03.12.1938, File No. I-35 of 1939, Police Department, Government of Orissa, pp. 1-2.

Appendix

Addition and Legalisation of a New Source of Income for the British: Water Revenue and Navigational Income

Ever since the British settled in India, they had always intended for maximizing revenue. It is already stated that the construction of Canals was one among many other policies of the British that brought them income. This canal project they did only in the areas where they can earn money. This endeavour gave them another way to exploit the peasants. Water revenue consisted of two kinds of incomes. Those were water rates and navigational charges. With time and tide it used to get fluctuated. For the collection of the revenue there was a revenue superintendent for canals.[1] The amount was fluctuated as the demand for water was determined by the availability of rain. Only during the period of scarcity (of water), the Orissa peasants opted for canal irrigation.

With the introduction of railway in Orissa by 1897-98, the water revenue particular in the field of navigational income declined in a larger extent. But still in the field of communication, the importance of canal remained intact.

Let us have a look at the income from the canal system to understand the importance of the same for the British.

Irrigational Income

In the year 1871-72, the total water rate collection was Rs. 17,915. Slowly it rose up to Rs. 19,071 in 1872-73. But in the very next year it declined to Rs. 17,412 in 1873-74 (as per 1873-74 report it was

Rs. 21,250).[2] The rates for water got modified and fixed for some years in 1873.[3] But in 1874-75, the total collection was Rs. 21,382 (but as per 1875-76 report it was Rs. 23612).[4] Followed by in 1875-76, the total water receipts excluding navigational income was Rs. 25,234 (as per 1876-77 report it was Rs. 25,022 and as per 1877-78 it was Rs. 25,234) against of Rs. 23,612 in 1874-75.[5] The income doubled in 1876-77 and amounted to Rs. 46,466.[6] The year 1877-78 had seen a high amount of water receipts comparing to preceding years. For the year, the income was Rs. 1,22,862 whereas the two preceding years income was Rs.46,466 for 1876-77 and it was Rs. 25,234 for 1875-76. It is not difficult to see that whenever, the State received scanty rainfall, the income increased from the canal irrigation.[7] Followed by in 1878-79, the income slightly declined to Rs. 1,21,804.[8]

So the total irrigational income for the last eight years from 1871-72 to 1878-79 were as follows (see Fig. 1):

1871-72	17915
1872-73	19071
1873-74	21250
1874-75	23612
1875-76	25234
1876-77	46466
1877-78	122862
1878-79	121804

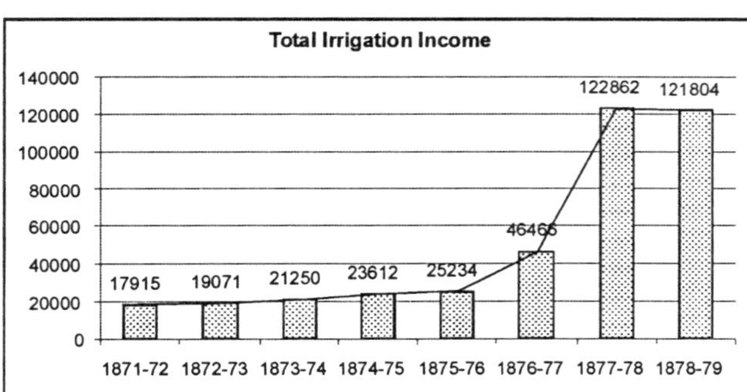

Fig. 1

Explanation

Figure 1 shows that there was an unhindered steady growth of the total irrigational income out of canal irrigation from 1871-72 to 1877-78 corresponding to the steady increase in the irrigated land. But the growth rate of this particular income from 1876-77 to 1877-78 was very high in comparing to other financial years. This was mainly attributed to the low rainfall during the period 1875-76 and 1877-78 that made the farmers to highly depend on the canal irrigation system.[9] From the chart, it can be concluded that the flow of income in the beginning – from 1871 to 1874 were remained almost same. However, from the period 1874-75, it gradually progressed and there was huge leap in the income between the period 1877- 78 and 1878-79. Therefore, the conclusion would be, the British had a comfortable income from the canal irrigation system at the cost of the peasants in Orissa.

In 1881-82, the irrigational realisation from Balasore alone was Rs. 2987 and from Cuttack it was much higher - Rs. 132267. But the very next year, from Balasore, the irrigational charges declined to Rs. 2056, because there was decline in the number of leases for canal water. But the same period, the collection from Cuttack had increased to Rs. 190118. This was due to the increase in the lease amount.[10] The next year the total realization declined to Rs. 124179 (for the year 1883-84). Out of which Rs.' 122403 from Cuttack alone, the rest was realized from Balasore (Rs. 1776).[11] The total income of the year 1884-85 was not available; but the recorded income from Balasore was Rs. 5814.[12] For 1885-86, the total irrigational income was Rs. 116939. While Cuttack contributed the majority – Rs. 111024; from Balasore city was Rs. 5915.[13] But the next year (for 1886-87), the total income came down to Rs. 105774.[14] During 1887-88 the amount reached to Rs. 138654.[15] But by the next year there was an increase of Rs. 17187 and the income reached to Rs. 156841.[16] During 1889-90, the income reached to Rs. 194716[17], whereas during 1890-91 it peaked to Rs. 249344.[18]

So the last ten years irrigational incomes were as follows (Fig. 2):

1881-82	135254
1882-83	192174
1883-84	124179
1884-85	NA
1885-86	116939
1886-87	105774
1887-88	138654
1888-89	156841
1889-90	194716
1890-91	249344

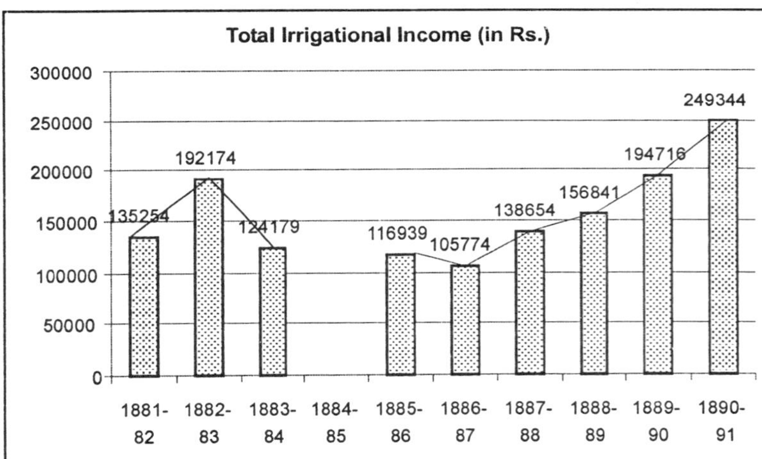

Fig. 2

Explanation

From the above chart, it is clear that comparing to 1878-79 irrigational income during 1881-82 was some extent higher. All of sudden it went up in the next financial years (1882-83). Despite good rainfall, around 1000 acres of additional land came under the canal system:

this was possible due to two reasons; the nature of lease system and apprehension about the rainfall, since the previous year it was bad. This contributed to the rise of water prices for short leased lands. This irrigational income slightly declined during the period 1883-84. And the income remained almost the same till 1886-87. From 1887-88 onwards, the income increased steadily and it peaked during the period 1890-91. Insufficient rainfall in the previous year (1889-90) also contributed the big leap.

The total collection from irrigation during the period 1892-93 was Rs. 104177; again it came down to Rs. 66390 by next year. Comparing to 1893-94, the income reached to Rs. 98058 during 1894-95.[19] The income again went up and reached to Rs. 202037 during 1895-96. In 1896-97, the income was Rs. 263420.[20] It again went to Rs. 314700 during 1897-98. The grand total of revenue from Canals for the period was Rs. 606900. But next year, the irrigational income came down to Rs. 272400. And the grand total of income from the canal also came down to Rs. 520500 during 1898-99.[21] Further it went down to Rs. 267978 during 1899-1900.[22] That income once again rose to Rs. 277812 during the period 1900-01.[23]

So, the last ten years income was:

1891-92	NA
1892-93	104177
1893-94	66390
1894-95	98058
1895-96	202037
1896-97	263420
1897-98	314700
1898-99	272400
1899-00	267978
1900-01	277812

A graphic presentation (Fig. 3) of the irrigational income for the period 1891-92 to 1900-01 is given on next page.

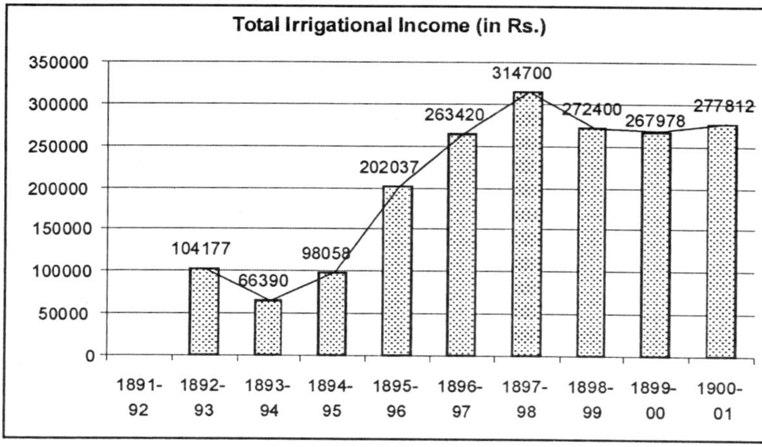

Fig. 3

Explanation

From the above chart it is clear that after 1890-91 this income came down, and the trend continued till 1893-94. The reasons behind it were the expiry of leases in 1892-93 and the rainfall during the said period was copious and well distributed.[24] Once again the income went up steadily from 1894-95 and touched the peak during 1897-98. This was owing to the resumption of leases for canal water in large number in the particular year[25] and also due to the drought that hit the period 1896-97.[26] Next financial year once again the income went down owing to the good rainfall. The irrigational income touched the highest in 1897-98 since the inception of the canal irrigation system.

In 1901-02, the income declined little bit to Rs. 239035. But by the next year it exceeded all preceding years' income and reached to Rs. 292262 during 1902-03. It further increased to Rs. 326485 in 1903-04. However in 1904-05, the income came down to Rs. 286717.[27]

During the financial year 1912-13, the total irrigational income was Rs. 425617.[28] The price hike of water to Rs. 11 contributed into it.[29] Though there was an increase in the income over the period from 1912-13 to 1920-21, the variations were not huge. During 1914-15 it was Rs. 442117 and further it increased to Rs. 451478 by the next financial year 1915-16.[30] The total irrigational income of the period 1916-17 was approximately, Rs. 460707[31]; a slight increase in the total revenue was recorded. However, the income declined to Rs. 452096 the very next year1917-18.[32] Next year by July 1919 once again the income rose to Rs. 483948 due to the increase in the amount of irrigated land.[33] The consecutive years–1919-20 and 1920-21–the recorded income was Rs. 496933 and Rs. 518882 respectively.[34]

The statistics of the income for the period between 1912-13 and 1920-21 is given below:

1911-12	NA
1912-13	425617
1913-14	NA
1914-15	442117
1915-16	451478
1916-17	460707
1917-18	452096
1918-19	483948
1919-20	496933
1920-21	518882

The graphic presentation (Fig. 4) of the income for the period between 1912-13 and 1920-21is given on next page.

Explanation

The graph shows that from 1912-13 to 1916-17, the income gradually and steadily increased. Though this could be attributed to the expansion of the irrigated land; a rise in the water rate to Rs. 3 was also contributed to the increase of revenue. There is marginal decrease recorded during the period 1917-18; this was due to the availability of a good rainfall.[35] But it picked up once again and resumed the growth.[36] By 1920-21, it peaked to Rs. 518882, that was the highest income recorded for the decade.

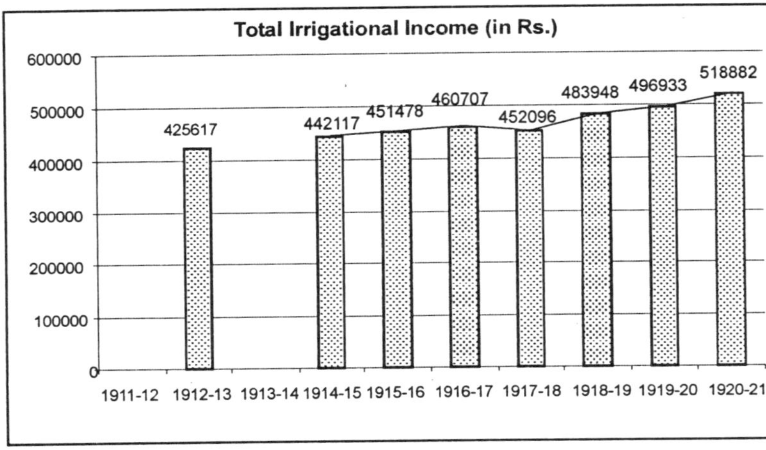

Fig. 4

Unfortunately, segregated data is not available for the combined income on the navigational and irrigational charges during the period. Hence, the combined data for Bihar and Orissa is used for the analysis. including both irrigation and navigational income of both the states, during 1929-30 the total revenue from the navigational and irrigational charges was Rs. 1788699. The next financial year- 1930-31, the amount declined to Rs. 1711000.[37] The 1931-32 period recorded a huge increase in the income compared to the previous year and the combined revenue for both Bihar and Orissa was Rs. 3865158.[38] In 1932-33 financial years, a slight decline was registered and the total income was Rs. 3684000.[39] The total amount of receipt, including both irrigation and navigational charges, which came from all canals of Bihar and Orissa province in 1933-34, was Rs. 3645480.[40] In the next financial year 1934-35, it increased to Rs. 3763000.[41] It went down again in 1935-36 to Rs. 2117000. [42] In 1936-37 the total irrigational revenue in Orissa was Rs. 567561. It went down some extent by the next financial year (1936-37) and reached to Rs. 546877, whereas in 1938-39 it was Rs. 410054.[43]

No data was available for the period from 1939-40 to 1946-47.

Navigational Income

Let us have a look at the navigational income. In 1871-72, the navigational income was Rs. 16,510 A and P8 (Anna for A and Paisa for P). Like irrigational income the navigational income also used to fluctuate from year to year. In 1872-73, the income declined to Rs. 10,044. In 1873-74 and 1874-75, the income recorded was Rs. 18,577 and Rs. 21,412 respectively.[44] But as per 1873-74 administration report the total navigational income was Rs. 23,104.[45] In 1875-76, the income was Rs. 16,112 against Rs. 19,358 last year (as per 1875-76 Report). The total mileage of navigable canal by July 1876 was 104 miles same as the previous year.[46]

Data was not available for the period between 1876-77 and 1877-78. The income for the year 1878-79 was Rs. 47,052. The income declined slightly to Rs. 46,489 and it further declined steeply to 34,643 in 1879-80. A slight improvement was marked next year with Rs. 39,087 for 1881-82. But in 1882-83 it increased considerably to Rs. 60,519.[47]

A graphic presentation (Fig. 5.) of the Navigational Income from 1831-32 to 1882-83 is given on the next page.

Explanation

Figure 5 indicates the marked fluctuation in the navigational income over a period of twelve years. As this was determined by the amount of traffic–both the government and the private traffic–it is logical to conclude that those periods for which the income was shown less was due to less traffic and *vice versa*. For instance the highest number of traffic was recorded in 1882-83 with 102706 traffic and correspondingly, the income was also highest with Rs. 60519 for the period. When the traffic came down to 86566 in 1878-79, the income reduced to Rs. 47052. Similarly, when the traffic further reduced to 75554 in 1879-80, the income also declined to Rs. 46489.[48]

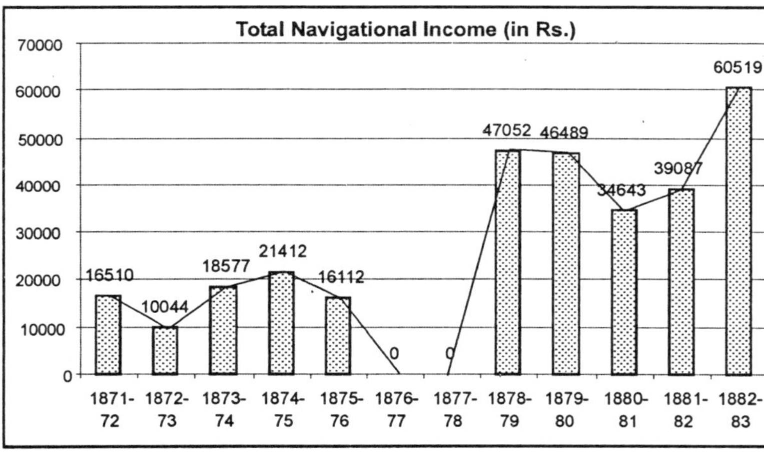

Fig. 5

During the year 1890-91, the total navigational income was Rs. 111709 correspondingly the traffic was also high for the period; 21937 boats sailed through the canals and a total 177 miles of canal open for irrigation and navigation.[49] The income for the period 1895-96 was Rs. 142617. And it further increased to Rs. 158262 for the period 1896-97.[50] The income reached to Rs. 211300 during 1897-98 periods and the total revenue from the canals also rose to Rs. 606900. It declined in the next year (during 1898-99) to Rs. 172700; the total revenue raised from the canals also deflated to Rs. 520500.[51] And it further went down to Rs. 147689 during 1899-1900.[52] It was the outcome of the introduction of railway for the first time in Orissa by 1898.[53]

Given below is the graphic presentation (Fig. 6) of the total navigational income from 1890-91 to 1899-1900.

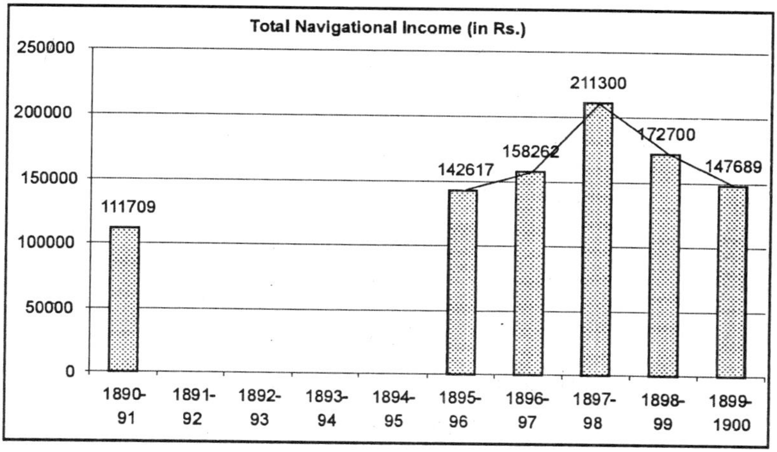

Fig. 6

Explanation

Figure 6 shows that the navigational income went up till 1897-98. Since then, it began to decline year by year. The extension of canals and the increased tempo of trade contributed to this trend till the introduction of railway in Orissa . But with the introduction of railway in Orissa, the income began to show a trend of decline. The income of 1897-98 was the highest income ever out of the navigational charges in Orissa.

In 1900-01, the total navigational income had gone down steeply from the period 1899-1900; from Rs. 147689 to Rs. 90485 owing to the newly introduced railway system. It gradually declined to Rs. 78153 in 1901-02 and further reduced to Rs. 68492 in 1902-03. There was slight improvement during the period 1903-04; the income went up to Rs. 70335. However, it went back to the earlier position in 1904-05 to Rs. 68698.[54]

In 1912-13 financial year, the total navigational income was Rs. 64959 against the last financial year's (1911-12) income Rs. 73690.[55] This decline took place mainly in the Taladanda and High Level Canal Range I. But the gross receipt from the Orissa Coast

Canal was Rs. 24834 for 1912-13 against Rs. 25061 of the preceding year.[56] After a year's gap in 1914-15, the income from navigational charges reached to Rs. 69906. By next year, in 1915-16, the income slightly, declined to Rs. 69253.[57] However for the last five years the average navigational revenue was around Rs. 70841. During 1916-17, the total income in this regards was Rs. 72268 which was little higher than the revenue of 1915-16. But further the revenue declined to Rs. 72036 by 1917-18.[58] Also the average went down to Rs. 70075. Once again that revenue declined to Rs. 71392 by 1918-19.[59] In the next financial year the revenue declined drastically to Rs. 58806.[60]

Figure 7 shows the graphic presentation of the navigational income for the period from 1911-12 to 1919-20.

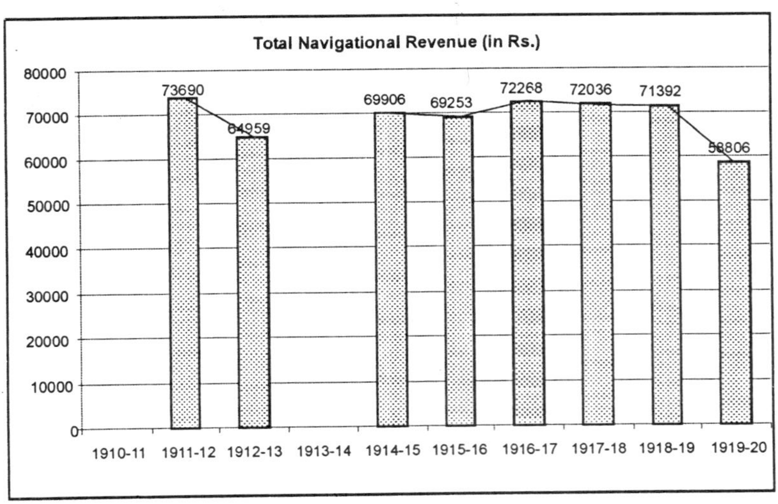

Fig. 7

Explanation

The graphs presented in Fig. 7 shows the variation in the navigational income for a period of ten years. It was already stated that the introduction of railway lines in Orissa affected the canal navigation adversely and so the income from that source. However, still it functioned as an important route for navigation from Orissa.

In 1920-21 financial year, the revenue declined by Rs. 18000 against the previous year's navigational income of Rs. 58896 to Rs. 49177. This was attributed to the hike in the navigational prices and the consequent low traffic and also nine canals were closed for a long period due the damage caused by a flood.[61] The income reached to little higher by 1926-27, as the total income of both Bihar and Orissa out of navigational income was Rs. 137566.[62] But once again the revenue of both the states declined to Rs. 124076 in 1927-28.[63] In 1929-30, the navigational revenue further declined by eighteen thousand rupees.[64] But as next year's record the amount was Rs. 1788699. However, the income once again declined to Rs. 1684000 by 1930-31.[65] Since segregated data is not available, we will not be able to a clear picture of the trend in income in Orissa. .

It is misfortune that we have no segregated data for Orissa from 1931 to 1934. Still as per the joint report of both the states in the financial year (1931-32), the income reduced to Rs. 115465, owing to the downfall in trade.[66] However, there was a slight improvement in 1932-33; the income reached to Rs. 116000.[67] Next year (1933-34), the income again went downward with Rs. 104811 owing to the general trade depression.[68] Data is not available for the period from 1934-35 to 1935-36.

According to Jadu Nath Mahapatra, for the year 1934-35, the total navigational income in the context of Orissa canal was Rs. 72916. The next year, it increased to Rs. 90264. In 1936-37, it declined to Rs. 69577 and further it declined to Rs. 64272 during 1937-38 periods. The revenue marginally went up in the next financial year (1938-39) to Rs. 67885.[69]

The total navigational income for the period 1934-35 to 1938-39 is given below in a graphic presentation (Fig. 8).

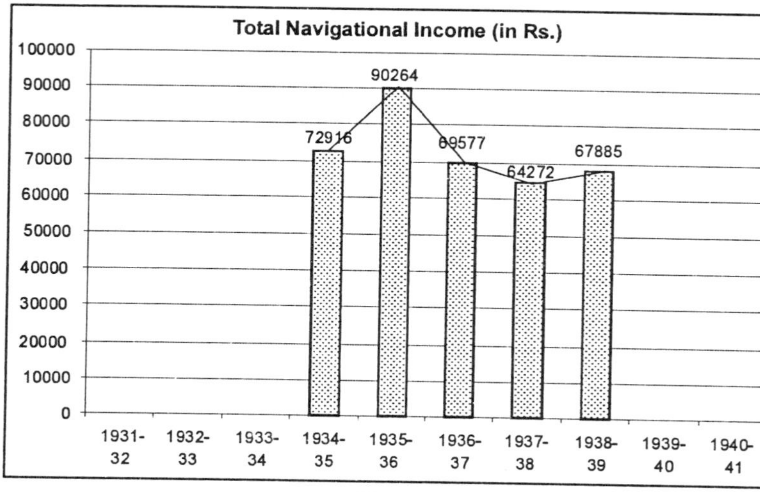

Fig. 8

Explanation

From the above presentation, it is clear that, even during the period 1938-39, the canal system played an important role in fetching income to the British, though the railways and the newly laid roads had taken away the glory of the canal system. The trade was resumed normal in 1935-36 after two years of general depression and it showed in the income too. However, it went to the previous position in the consecutive years. Unfortunately, we do not have records for the period from 1939-40 to 1946-47 in this regard. Probably there would not have any considerable progress in the commerce and trade sectors as this era was marked with two big events: the World War II period and Quit India movement. But it can safely be concluded that the railway brought down the importance of the canal traffic considerably.

Notes

1. A General Administration Report on Orissa Division: 1872-1873, Cuttack, 1873, p. 33.
2. A General Administration Report on Orissa Division: 1874-1875, Cuttack, 1875, p. 13.
3. A General Administration Report on Orissa Division: 1872-1873, Cuttack, 1873, p. 33.
4. A General Administration Report on Orissa Division: 1874-1875, Cuttack, 1875, p. 13.
5. A General Administration Report on Orissa Division: 1875-1876, Cuttack, 1876, p. 15.
6. A General Administration Report on Orissa Division: 1876-1877, Cuttack, 1877, p. 14.
7. Annual General Administration Report, Orissa Division, for 1877-78, Cuttack, 1878, p. 31.
8. Annual General Report, Orissa Division for 1878-79, Cuttack, 1879, p. 39.
9. Annual General Administration Report, Orissa Division, for 1877-78, Cuttack, 1878, p. 31.
10. Annual General Report, Orissa Division, for 1882-83, Cuttack, 1883, p. 52-54.
11. Annual General Report, Orissa Division, for 1883-84, Cuttack, 1884, p. 36.
12. Annual General Administration Report of the Orissa Division, for 1884-85, Cuttack, 1885, p. 41.
13. Annual General Administration Report of the Orissa Division, for 1885-86, Cuttack, 1886, p. 44.
14. Annual General Administration Report of the Orissa Division, for 1886-87, Cuttack, 1887, p. 41.
15. Annual General Administration Report of the Orissa Division, for 1887-88, Cuttack, 1888, p. 34.
16. Annual General Administration Report of the Orissa Division, for 1888-89, Cuttack, 1889, p. 39.
17. Annual General Administration Report of the Orissa Division, for 1889-90, Cuttack, 1890, p. 18.
18. Annual General Administration Report of the Orissa Division, for 1890-91, Cuttack, 1891, p. 14.

19. Annual General Administration Report of the Orissa Division for 1894-95, Cuttack, 1895, p. 49.
20. Patnaik, Gorachand. *The Famine and Some Aspects of the British Economic Policy in Orissa*, 1866-1905, Vidyapuri Publication, Cuttack, 1980, p. 117.
21. Maddox, S.L. Final Report on the Survey and Settlement of the Province of Orissa, 1890 to 1900, Government of Bengal, Calcutta, 1900, p. 92.
22. Annual General Administration Report of the Orissa Division, for 1899-1900, Cuttack, 1900, p. 32.
23. Quinquennial Adm. Report of the Orissa Division from 1900-01 to 1904-05, Government of Bengal, Calcutta, p. 37.
24. Annual General Administration Report of the Orissa Division, for 1894-95, Cuttack, 1895, p. 49.
25. Annual General Administration Report of the Orissa Division, for 1897-98, Cuttack, 1898, p. 39.
26. Annual General Administration Report of the Orissa Division, for 1899-1900, Cuttack, 1900, p. 31.
27. Quinquennial Adm. Report of the Orissa Division from 1900-01 to 1904-05, Government of Bengal, Calcutta, p. 37.
28. Report on the Administration of Bihar and Orissa, 1912-13, Government of Bihar and Orissa, Patna, 1914, p. 71.
29. *Ibid.*
30. Report on the Administration of Bihar and Orissa, 1915-16, Government of Bihar and Orissa, Patna, 1917, p. 69.
31. Report on the Administration of Bihar and Orissa, 1917-18, Government of Bihar and Orissa, Patna, 1919, pp. 74-75.
32. *Ibid.*
33. Report on the Administration of Bihar and Orissa, 1918-19, Government of Bihar and Orissa, Patna, 1920, p. 76.
34. Report on the Administration of Bihar and Orissa, 1920-21, Government of Bihar and Orissa, Patna, 1922, p. 27.
35. Report on the Administration of Bihar and Orissa 1917-18, Government of Bihar and Orissa, 1919, Patna, p. 74.
36. Report on the Administration of Bihar and Orissa 1918-19, Government of Bihar and Orissa, 1920, Patna, p. 76.
37. Mansfield. P.T., *Bihar and Orissa in 1930-31*, Government of Bihar and Orissa, Patna, 1932, Appendix III.

38. Williams, R.A.E., *Bihar and Orissa in 1931-32*, Government of Bihar and Orissa, Patna, 1933, p. 32.
39. Gupta. R.L., *Bihar and Orissa in 1932-33*, Government of Bihar and Orissa, Patna, 1934, p. 85.
40. Wilcock. J.S., *Bihar and Orissa in 1933-34*, Government of Bihar and Orissa, Patna, 1935, p. 91.
41. Solomon. S., *Bihar and Orissa in 1934-35*, Government of Bihar and Orissa, Patna, 1935, p. 122.
42. Narayan, Sahib Kailaspati, *Bihar and Orissa in 1935-36*, Government of Bihar and Orissa, Patna, 1938, p. 27.
43. Mahapatra, Jadu Nath, *Orissa in 1936-37 to 1938-39*, Government of Orissa, Cuttack, 1941, p. 132.
44. A General Administration Report on Orissa Division: 1874-1875, Cuttack, 1875, p. 13.
45. A General Administration Report on Orissa Division: 1873-1874, Cuttack, 1874, p. 15.
46. Annual General Administration Report on Orissa Division: 1875-1876, Cuttack, 1876, p. 17.
47. Annual General Report, Orissa Division, for 1882-83, Cuttack, 1883, p. 20.
48. *Ibid.*
49. Report on the Administration of Bengal, 1890-91, Government of Bengal, Calcutta, 1891, p. 24.
50. Quinquennial Adm. Report of the Orissa Division from 1900-01 to 1904-05, Government of Bengal, Calcutta, p. 37.
51. Maddox, S.L., Final Report on the Survey and Settlement of the Province of Orissa, 1890-1900, Government of Bengal, Calcutta, 1900, p. 93.
52. Quinquennial Adm. Report of the Orissa Division from 1900-01 to 1904-05, Government of Bengal, Calcutta, p. 37.
53. Annual General Administration Report of the Orissa Division, for 1899-1900, Cuttack, 1900, p. 11 and Patnaik, Gorachand. *The Famine and Some Aspects of the British Economic Policy in Orissa*, 1866-1905, Vidyapuri Publication, Cuttack, 1980, pp. 116-117.
54. Quinquennial Adm. Report of the Orissa Division from 1900-01 to 1904-05, Government of Bengal, Calcutta, p. 37.
55. Report on the Administration of Bihar and Orissa, 1912-1913, Government of Bihar and Orissa, Patna, 1914, p. 71.
56. *Ibid.*, p. 72.

57. Report on the Administration of Bihar and Orissa, 1915-1916, Government of Bihar and Orissa, Patna, 1917, p. 69.
58. Report on the Administration of Bihar and Orissa, 1917-1918, Government of Bihar and Orissa, Patna, 1919, p. 75.
59. Report on the Administration of Bihar and Orissa, 1918-1919, Government of Bihar and Orissa, Patna, 1920, p. 77. And Report on the Administration of Bihar and Orissa 1919-1920, Government of Bihar and Orissa, Patna, 1921, p. 62.
60. Report on the Administration of Bihar and Orissa, 1919-1920, Government of Bihar and Orissa, Patna, 1921, p. 62.
61. Report on the Administration of Bihar and Orissa, 1920-1921, Government of Bihar and Orissa, Patna, 1922, p. 27
62. Grahm Lacey, W., *Bihar and Orissa in 1926-27*, Government of Bihar and Orissa, Patna, 1928, p. 92.
63. *Bihar and Orissa in 1927-28*, Government of Bihar and Orissa, Patna, 1929, p. 83.
64. Jagmohan, R., *Bihar and Orissa in 1929-30*, Government of Bihar and Orissa, Patna, 1931, p. 93.
65. Mansfield, P.T., *Bihar and Orissa in 1930-31*, Government of Bihar and Orissa, Patna, 1932, Appendix III.
66. Williams. R.A.E., *Bihar and Orissa in 1931-32*, Government of Bihar and Orissa, Patna, 1933, p. 32.
67. Gupta. R.L., *Bihar and Orissa in 1933-34*, Government of Bihar and Orissa, Patna, 1935, p. 91.
68. Wilcock. J.S., *Bihar and Orissa in 1932-33*, Government of Bihar and Orissa, Patna, 1934, p. 85.
69. Mahapatra, JaduNath, *Orissa in 1936-37 to 1938-39*, Government of Orissa, Cuttack, p. 132.

Bibliography

Primary Sources

Government Reports—Annual

Annual Report on Survey and Settlement, Departments under the control of Directorate of the Department of Land Records and Surveys, Bihar and Orissa for the Year ending 30th September, 1924, Government of Bihar and Orissa, Patna, 1925.

Bihar and Orissa in 1927-28, Government of Bihar and Orissa, Patna, 1929.

General Review of the Administration of the Orissa States for the Year 1931-32, Government of India Press, Calcutta, 1932.

Gupta, R.L., *Bihar and Orissa in 1932-33*, Government of Bihar and Orissa, Patna, 1934.

Jagamohan, R., *Bihar and Orissa in 1929-30*, Government of Bihar and Orissa, Patna, 1931.

Kailaspati Narayan, R.S., *Bihar, and Orissa in 1935-36*, Government of Bihar and Orissa, Patna, 1938.

Lacey, W.G., *Bihar and Orissa in 1926-27*, Government of Bihar and Orissa, Patna, 1928.

Maddox, S.L., *Final Report on the Survey and Settlement of the Province of Orissa, 1890-1900*, Vol. I, Government of Bengal, Calcutta, 1900.

Mansfield, P.T., *Bihar and Orissa in 1930-31*, Government of Bihar and Orissa, Patna, 1932.

Report on the Administration of Bengal, 1910-1911, Government of Bengal, Calcutta, 1912.

Report on the Administration of Bihar and Orissa, 1912-1913, Government of Bihar and Orissa, Patna, 1914.
Report on the Administration of Bihar and Orissa, 1915-1916, Government of Bihar and Orissa, Patna, 1917.
Report on the Administration of Bihar and Orissa, 1917-1918, Government of Bihar and Orissa, Patna, 1919.
Report on the Administration of Bihar and Orissa, 1918-1919, Government of Bihar and Orissa, Patna, 1920.
Report on the Administration of Bihar and Orissa, 1919-1920, Government of Bihar and Orissa, Patna, 1921.
Report on the Administration of Bihar and Orissa, 1920-1921, Government of Bihar and Orissa, Patna, 1922.
Season and Crop Report of Orissa for the year 1944-45, Government of Orissa, Cuttack, 1946
Season and Crop Report of Orissa for the year, 1939-40, Government of Orissa, Cuttack, 1941.
Season and Crop Report of Orissa for the year, 1941-42, Government of Orissa, Cuttack, 1943.
Season and Crop Report of Orissa for the year, 1943-44, Government of Orissa, Cuttack, 1945.
Season and Crop Report of Orissa for the year, 1945-46, Government of Orissa, Cuttack, 1947.
Solomon, S., 1937, *Bihar and Orissa in 1934-35*, Government of Bihar and Orissa, Patna.
Wasi. S.M., 1942, *Bihar in 1938-39*, Government of Bihar, Patna.
Wilcock., J.S., 1935, *Bihar and Orissa in 1933-34*, Government of Bihar and Orissa, Patna.
Williams, R.A.E., 1933, *Bihar and Orissa in 1931-32*, Government of Bihar and Orissa, Patna.

Government Reports—General

A Short Summery of the Administration of Orissa in 1936.
Agricultural Statistics of Orissa, for 1939-40, Government of Orissa, Cuttack, 1943.
General Administration Report on Orissa Division: 1872-1873, Commissioner of the Orissa Division, Government of Bengal, Cuttack, 1873.

General Administration Report on Orissa Division: 1873-1874, Commissioner of the Orissa Division, Government of Bengal, Cuttack, 1874.

General Administration Report on Orissa Division: 1874-1875, Commissioner of the Orissa Division, Government of Bengal, Cuttack, 1875.

General Administration Report on Orissa Division: 1875-1876, Commissioner of the Orissa Division, Government of Bengal, Cuttack, 1876.

General Administration Report on Orissa Division: 1876-1877, Commissioner of the Orissa Division, Government of Bengal, Cuttack, 1877.

Annual General Administration Report, Orissa Division for, 1877-78, Commissioner of the Orissa Division, Government of Bengal, Cuttack, 1878.

Annual General Administration Report of the Orissa Division, for 1884-85, Commissioner of the Orissa Division, Government of Bengal, Cuttack, 1885.

Annual General Administration Report of the Orissa Division, for 1885-86, Commissioner of the Orissa Division, Government of Bengal, Cuttack, 1886.

Annual General Administration Report of the Orissa Division, for 1886-87, Commissioner of the Orissa Division, Government of Bengal, Cuttack, 1887.

Annual General Administration Report of the Orissa Division, for 1887-88, Commissioner of the Orissa Division, Government of Bengal, Cuttack, 1888.

Annual General Administration Report of the Orissa Division, for 1888-89, Commissioner of the Orissa Division, Government of Bengal, Cuttack, 1889.

Annual General Administration Report of the Orissa Division, for 1889-90, Commissioner of the Orissa Division, Government of Bengal, Cuttack, 1890.

Annual General Administration Report of the Orissa Division, for 1890-91, Commissioner of the Orissa Division, Government of Bengal, Cuttack, 1891.

Annual General Administration Report of the Orissa Division, for 1894-95, Commissioner of the Orissa Division, Government of Bengal, Cuttack, 1895.

Annual General Administration Report of the Orissa Division, for 1897-98, Commissioner of the Orissa Division, Government of Bengal, Cuttack, 1898.

Annual General Administration Report of the Orissa Division, for 1899-1900, Commissioner of the Orissa Division, Government of Bengal, Cuttack, 1900.

Annual General Report, Orissa Division, for 1878-79, Commissioner of the Orissa Division, Government of Bengal, Cuttack, 1879.

Annual General Report, Orissa Division, for 1882-83, Commissioner of the Orissa Division, Government of Bengal, Cuttack, 1883.

Annual General Report, Orissa Division, for 1883-84, Commissioner of the Orissa Division, Government of Bengal, Cuttack, 1884.

Annual Report on the Administration of the Bengal Presidency: 1860-1861, Government of Bengal, Calcutta, 1861.

Bihar and Orissa First Decennial Review, 1912-1922, Government of Bihar, and Orissa, Patna, 1923.

Mahapatra, Jadu Nath, 1941 *Orissa in 1936-37 to 1938-39,* Government of Orissa, Cuttack.

Owen, G.E., 1922 *Bihar and Orissa in 1921,* Government of Bihar and Orissa, Patna.

Report of the Indian Famine Commission, 1901 and Papers Relating Thereto, Government of England, London, 1901.

Report of the Indian Irrigation Commission, 1901-03.

Report of the Irrigation Rates Revision Committee, Revenue Department, Government of Orissa, 1967.

Report of the Land Revenue Administration of the Lower Provinces for the Year 1906-1907, Government of Bengal, Calcutta, 1907.

Report on the Administration of Bengal, 1890-91, Government of Bengal, Calcutta, 1891.

Report on the Administration of Bengal, 1910-1911, Government of Bengal, Calcutta, 1912.

Report on the Land Revenue Administration of the Districts of North Orissa for the Year 1944-45, Government of Orissa, Cuttack, 1947.

Report on the Land Revenue Administration of the Districts of North Orissa for the Year 1946-47, Government of Orissa, Cuttack, 1948.

Report on the Land Revenue Administration of the Lower Provinces for the Official Year 1861-1862, Savielle and Cranenburgh Printers, Bengal Printing Company Limited, Calcutta, 1862.

Report on the Land Revenue Administration of the Lower Provinces for the Official Year 1862-1863, Government of Bengal, Calcutta, 1863.

Report on the Land Revenue Administration of the Lower Provinces for the Official Year 1863-1864, O.T. Cutter, Military Orphan Press, Calcutta, 1864.

Report on the Land Revenue Administration of the Lower Provinces for the Official Year 1864-1865, H. Dean, Calcutta Central Press Company Limited, 5, Council House Street, Calcutta, 1865.

Report on the Land Revenue Administration of the Lowe, Provinces for the Year 1907-1908, Government of Bengal, Calcutta, 1908.

Report on the Land Revenue Administration of the Lower Provinces for the Year 1908-1909, Government of Bengal, Calcutta, 1909.

Selections from the Records of the Government of India in the P.W.D. No. CCIV, P.W.D. Serial No. 3, Papers relating to the Orissa Coast Canal, Government of India, Calcutta, 1885.

The Famine Inquiry Commission, Final Report, Government of India, Delhi, 1945.

District Gazetteers

Balasore District Gazetteer Statistics, 1900-01 to 1910-11, Government of Bihar and Orissa Press, Patna, 1915.

Hunter. W.W., 1885 *The Imperial Gazetteer of India, Balasore to Biramhanta,* Vol. II, Trubner & Co. London.

O'Malley. L.S.S., 1933, *Bihar and Orissa District Gazetteers, Cuttack,* Government of Bihar and Orissa, New Delhi: Losos Press.

O'Malley. L.S.S., 1929, *Bihar and Orissa District Gazetteers, Puri,* Government of Bihar and Orissa, New Delhi: Losos Press.

Puri District Gazetteer Statistics, 1900-01 to 1910-11, Government of Bihar and Orissa, Patna, 1915.

Puri District Gazetteer Statistics, 1900-02, Government of Bihar and Orissa, Patna, 1905.

Secondary Sources

Bagchi, Amiya Kumar. (October 1992) Land Tax, Property Rights and Peasant Insecurity in Colonial India, *The Journal of Peasant Studies,* Vol. 20, No.1, pp. 1-49.

Bandyopadhyay, S. (2013). *From Plassey to Partition, A History of Modern India.* New Delhi: Orient Blackswan Private Limited.

Barik, S. (2013). *British Economic Policy: A Study in Historical Perspective.* Kolkata: Punthi Pustak.

Behera, A.K. (1997). *Irrigation in British Orissa.* (N.R. Patnaik, Ed.) New Delhi: Indus Publishing Company.

Bhata, B.B. (1997). *The Natural Calamities in Orissa in the 19th Century.* New Delhi: Commonwealth Publishers.

Bhola, S.C. (1990). *British Economic Policy in Orissa (1905-1947).* New Delhi: Discovery Publishing House.

Chandra, B. (1987). *Nationalism and Colonialism in Modern India,* New Delhi: Orient Longman.

Chandra, B. (1999). *Essays on Colonialism.* New Delhi: Orient Blackswan Private Limited.

Chandra, B. (March 1968) "Reinterpretation of Nineteenth Century Indian Economic History", *IESHR,* 5 (1).

Chaudhury, Pradipta. (Aug-Sep., 1991). "Peasants and British Rule in Orissa", *Social Scientist,* Vol. 19, No. 8/9.

Chittibabu, D. (2004). *Mitigation of Flooding and Cyclone Hazard in Orissa, India.* Nat: Haz.

D'Souza, R. (1998). *The Deltaic Rivers of the Bengal Presidency: The Political Economy of Flood Control in Orissa.* Unpublished work.

D'Souza, R. (2013). *Drowned and Damned: Colonial Capitalism and Flood Control in Eastern India.* New Delhi: Oxford University Press, India.

Darley, B. (1941, December 12). "The Development of Irrigation in India", *Journal of the Royal Society of Arts,* Vol. 90 (No. 4602), pp. 39-56.

Das, B.S. (1976, June). "Orissa's Economy in the Nineteenth Century", *Social Scientist,* Vol. 4 (No. 11).

Das, P.C. (1989). *The Economic History of Orissa in the 19th Century.* New Delhi: Commonwealth Publisher.

Das, S. Binod (1976). "Orissa's Economy in the Nineteenth Century", *Social Scientist,* Vol. 4, No. 11, Jun., 1976.

Gadgil, D.R. (1972). *The Industrial Evolution in India in the Recent Times,* Delhi: Oxford University Press.

Gilmartin, D. (1994, Nov.). "Scientific Empire and Imperial Science: Colonialism and Irrigation Technology in the Indus Basin", *The Journal of Asian Studies,* 53(4): 1127-1149.

Grover, B.L. and Grover, S. (2008). *A New Look at Modern Indian History.* New Delhi: S. Chand & Company Ltd.

Guha, Ranajit, (1982). *A Rule of Property for Bengal: An Essay on the Idea of Permanent Settlement,* New Delhi: Orient Longman.

Habib, I. (1975, March). "Colonization of the Indian Economy, 1757-1900", *Social Scientist,* 3(8): 23-53.

Habib, I. (2006). *Indian Economy (1858-1914).* Chennai: Tulika Publication.

Hardiman, D. (1998, June 20-26). "Well Irrigaton in Gujarat: Systems of Use, Hierarchies of Control", *Economic and Political Weekly,* 33(25): 1533-1544.

Hunter, W. (1872). *Orissa* (Vol. II). London: Smith, Elder & Co., 15, Waterloo Place.

Jena, K. (1968). *Land Revenue Administration in Orissa During the Nineteenth Century.* New Delhi: S. Chand & Co.

Macpherson, W.J. (2013). Economic Development in India under the British Crown, 1858-1947, (A.J. Youngson, Ed.), *Economic Developments in the Long Run,* London: Routledge.

Mishra, D.B. (2011). *Concise History of Orissa.* New Delhi: Kalyani Publishers.

Mohapatra, J. (1941). *Orissa in 1936-37 to 1938-39.* Cuttack: Government Press.

Mukherjee, M., (2005). *Colonizing Agriculture: The Myth of Punjab Exceptionalism,* Vol IX. New Delhi: Sage Publications India Private Limited.

Mukherjee, Nilmani (1962) *Ryotwari System in Madras 1792 1827,* Calcutta: K.L. Mukhopadhyay.

Narain, A.A. (1997). *Dying Wisdom: Rise, Fall and Potential of India's Traditional Water Harvesting.* New Delhi: Centre for Science and Environment.

Nayak, G. (May-June, 2010). *The Coast Canal in Orissa During the Colonial Era,* Orissa Review.

Panda, H. (2014). *History of Odisha.* Cuttack: Kitab Mahal.

Panda, S.K. (1991). *Medieval Orissa:, A Socio-Economic Study.* New Delhi: Mittal Publications.

Pany, R.K. and Pani, K.K. (2015). *Odisha Economy.* Cuttack: Kitab Mahal.

Patnaik, G. (1980). *The Famine and some aspects of the British Economic Policy in Orissa (1866-1905).* Cuttack: Vidyapuri.

Pradhan, N. (2010). *Gangadhar Granthavali, Krushak Samgita, Krushakara Atmakatha* (Odia book). Cuttack: Dharmagrantha Publication.

Rao, G.N. (1985, June 22-29). "Transition from Subsistence to Commercialised Agriculture: A Study of Krishna District of Andhra", *Economic and Political Weekly,* Vol. 20 (No. 25/26), A60-A69.

Ray, P.K. (2010). *Kendrapara Zilla Itihasa Second Part.* Bhubaneswar: Pachima Publication.

Reddy, M.A. (1990, March 24). "Travails of an Irrigation Company in South India", *Economic and Political Weekly,* Vol. 25 (no. 12), 619-621+623-628.

Reddy, V.R. (1990, May 5-12). "Irrigation in Colonial India: A Study of Madras Presidency during 1860-1900". *Economic and Political Weekly,* Vol. 25, (No. 18/19), 1047-1054.

Roy, T. (2000). *Economic History of India (1857-1947).* New Delhi: Oxford Press.

Sahoo, R. (1997). *Agricultural Development in British Orissa.* (N.R. Patnaik, Ed.) New Delhi: Indus Publishing House.

Sahoo, R.L. (2004). *Agrarian Change and Peasant Unrest in Colonial India, Orissa 1912-1939,* New Delhi: Manak Publication.

Samal, J.K. (1990). *Economic History of Orissa (1866-1912).* New Delhi: Mittal Publications.

Samal, J.K. (1993). *Agrarian History of Orissa Under the British Rule.* Delhi: Kanishka Publishers Distributors.

Samal, J.K. (2000). *Economic History of Colonial Orissa, 1866-1947.* New Delhi: Munshiram Manoharlal Publishers Pvt. Ltd.

Senapati, F.M. (1963-1965). *Fakir Mohan Granthavali.* Cuttack: Friends Publishers.

Sengupta, N. (1985, November). "Irrigation: Traditional vs. Modern", *Economic and Political Weekly,* Vol. 20 (No. 45/47), 1919-1921+1923-1925+1927+1929-1931+1933+1935+1937-1938.

Sengupta, S. (2000, December 30). "Political Economy of Irrigation: Tanks in Orissa, 1850-1996". *Economic and Political Weekly, 333333* (11111), 4695-4700.

Stokes, Eric (1992). *English Utilitarians and India,* Delhi: Oxford University Press.

Stone, I. (1984). *Canal Irrigation in British India: Perspectives on Technological Change in a Peasant Economy.* London: Cambridge University Press.

Thorner, D. (1956). *Agrarian Prospect in India.* Delhi: University Press.

Vera, Anstey (1931). *The Economic Development of India.* London: Longmans, Green & Co.

Vijay Kumar, T. (1998). "Canal Irrigation under Godavari and Kistna Anicuts during Second Half of 19th Century: Certain Disadvantages", *Itihas,* Vol. XXIII (1 & 2): 115-24.

Vijay Kumar, T. (2015), "Irrigation Politics and the Anicuts in Andhra", In: Adapa Satyanarayan, (Ed.), *Early Modern Andhra Hyderabad and Company Rule AD 1724-1857,* Hyderabad: Emesco Books.

Whitcombe, E. (1984). "Irrigation", In: D. Kumar, and M. Desai (Ed.), *The Cambridge Economic History of India* (Vol. II, pp. 677-737). New Delhi: Orient Longman Private Limited.

Wilson, H.M. (1903). *Irrigation in India.* Uknown Publisher.

News papers

The Samaj, Balasore, 14th November, 2016, p. 9.

The Samaj, Balasore, 13th April, 2017, p. 6.

Web sources

URL: https://aelarsen.wordpress.com/tag/enrico-lo-verso/(Accessed on 6/6/2017)

URL: https://aelarsen.wordpress.com/tag/renzo-martinelli/ (Accessed on 6/6/2017)

URL: http://understandingsociety.blogspot.in/2009/05/longue-duree.html (Accessed on 8/6/2017)

URL: http://www.thehindu.com/opinion/op-ed/what-is-longue-dure-in-historiography/article18159741.ece (Accessed on 8/6/2017)

Index